The Resistible Rise
of Arturo Ui

Works of Bertolt Brecht
published by
Arcade

Baal

The Caucasian Chalk Circle

Collected Stories

The Good Person of Szechwan

*The Good Person of Szechwan, Mother Courage and Her
Children,* and *Fear and Misery of the Third Reich*

Life of Galileo

Life of Galileo, The Resistible Rise of Arturo Ui,
and *The Caucasian Chalk Circle*

Man Equals Man and *The Elephant Calf*

The Measures Taken and other Lehrstücke

Mother Courage and Her Children

Mother Courage and Her Children, adapted by David Hare

Mr. Puntila and His Man Matti

The Resistible Rise of Arturo Ui

The Rise and Fall of the City of Mahagonny
and *The Seven Deadly Sins of the Petty Bourgeoisie*

Saint Joan of the Stockyards

Schweyk in the Second World War and *The Visions of
Simone Machard*

The Threepenny Opera

The Threepenny Opera, Baal, and *The Mother*

BERTOLT BRECHT

The Resistible Rise
of Arturo Ui

Translated by Ralph Manheim

Edited by John Willett and Ralph Manheim

ARCADE PUBLISHING•NEW YORK

FIRST ARCADE PAPERBACK EDITION 2001

The Resistible Rise of Arturo Ui, originally published in German under
the title *Der aufhaltsame Aufstieg des Arturi Ui*, was first published in
this translation in 1981.

ISBN 1-55970-543-4
Library of Congress Catalog Card Number 00-135896
Library of Congress Cataloging-in-Publication information is available.

Published in the United States of America by Arcade Publishing, Inc., New
York
Distributed by Time Warner Trade Publishing

10 9 8 7 6 5 4 3 2 1

CCP

PRINTED IN THE UNITED STATES OF AMERICA

CAUTION

Contents

Introduction

The Resistible Rise of Arturo Ui is, on the face of it, something of
a sport among Brecht's dramatic works. Written during World
War II when Hitler was at the height of his power, it is the last
of those great plays of Brecht's Scandinavian exile whose rich
variety led him to note that

> the plays tend to fly apart like constellations in the new physics,
> as though here too some kind of dramaturgical core had
> exploded.

True as this is of his oeuvre from *Fear and Misery of the Third
Reich* (1937–38) right up to his departure for America in May
1941, *Ui* was perhaps the most clearly centrifugal of them all, for
it was dashed off as an afterthought in a mere three weeks following the completion of *Puntila* and *The Good Person of Szechwan*
while his household was waiting in Helsinki for United States
visas to come through. Conceived with a view to the American
stage – Brecht did not envisage any German-language production
at the time – it seems like an unplanned, high-spirited appendix
to his most isolated, yet also most fruitful years.

Only two months earlier, in March 1941, the American stage
designer Mordecai Gorelik had sent Brecht a copy of his book
New Theatres for Old, a general survey of the modern theatre
whose emphasis on the 'epic' approach owed much to Brecht's
ideas. Before that, in 1935, when the playwright had paid his only
prewar visit to the U.S., Gorelik's sets had provided the one
redeeming feature of that New York production of *The Mother*
which Brecht and Hanns Eisler had vainly tried to direct along
their own lines; since then Gorelik had visited the Brechts in
Denmark and been invited to form part of that Diderot Society or
'Society for Theatrical Science' which Brecht was hoping to set
up as an antidote to the Stanislavsky-based 'Method' style of

naturalistic acting. Now, reading Gorelik's book and reconsidering the possibilities of the epic (or loosely narrative) structure – thinking no doubt also about the American theatre and his own possible role in it – Brecht was transported back to his earlier American experiences and

> again struck by the idea i once had in new york, of writing a gangster play that would recall certain events familiar to us all. (*the gangster play we know.*)

– this last phrase being set down in English, a language in which he would increasingly have to think.

Executive as ever, within a few days he had sketched out the plan of the play, noting in his journal that 'of course it will have to be written in the grand style'. That was on 10 March. On the 28th – 'in the midst of all the commotion about visas and the chances of our making the journey' – the play was complete except for the last scene. Then four days later he was already looking back at the finished job and starting to revise it. He was worried mainly about the imperfections of his 'grand style' blank verse, which he had at first written without paying too much attention to niceties of metre and scansion, partly (he claimed) because the play was anyway not going to be performed in German; partly on the grounds that a certain metrical raggedness would accord well with the crudity of the gangster characters. His collaborator Margarete Steffin was able to convince him that this was only an excuse for slipshod writing, whose faults might well stimulate a similar carelessness in the putative translator.

There was not time to do much – there was none of the usual prolonged rewriting – and by the middle of April the script was ready for submission to American producers. Soon after that the long-awaited visas arrived and on 13 May the family set off for neighbouring Leningrad, then Moscow, Vladivostok, the Philippines and points east. Brecht by that time had learnt of the success of the Zurich production of *Mother Courage*: this being the first staging of any of the big Scandinavian plays. *Galileo* and *The Good Person of Szechwan* had gone off to the same theatre, though the former was primarily intended for New York and, along with the *Fear and Misery* sketches, had already been translated by Brecht's German-American friend Ferdinand Reyher. Of this remarkable batch only *Puntila* seems not to have

struck Brecht as a possible work for the United States; he
evidently thought of it as primarily for Finnish consumption,
though the Finns' impending alliance with Nazi Germany soon
put paid to any chance of that. As for *Ui*, it 'ought really to stand
a chance on the U.S. stage', so he told Gorelik, and he had clearly
enjoyed himself writing it. Once again – and for the last time – he
had returned to the largely mythical America of his earlier plays,
filling it out with his and his family's accumulated knowledge of
gangster movies and lore, and linking it to unremitting ridicule of
the still victorious Nazis. In this critical moment of history –
critical not only for the world but also for his own safety – he had
reacted by writing very largely for fun.

*   *   *

Brecht's obsession with the American setting – and specifically
with Chicago – was an old one, going right back to the writing
of his third play *In the Jungle* and of the poem 'Epistle to the
Chicagoans' in the chilly Berlin of winter 1921–22. Starting as a
form of fashionable exoticism, with strange underworld characters called Skinny, Worm and Baboon snuffling around in front
of a backdrop largely derived from Upton Sinclair, it served even
then as a cloak to distance German audiences from what were
really parables about their own society. By the end of the 1920s
the device was no longer quite so effective, and Brecht on second
thoughts joined with Weill to have the American names in their
opera *Mahagonny* replaced by German ones. None the less his
preoccupation with the U.S. survived his conversion to
Marxism, to take on a new socio-economic emphasis as he began
studying the great capitalist trusts and tycoons, immortalised by
him in the Faustian character of the millionaire Pierpont Mauler
in *St Joan of the Stockyards*. By then the gangster world too had
begun to fascinate him, thanks no doubt to his addictive reading
of crime stories, and something of this fascination seeped into
the London world of *The Threepenny Opera*, where gangster and
businessman were shown to be brothers under the skin, linked
by the same unscrupulous morality. A year later the same recipe
was less successfully repeated in *Happy End*, though here the
setting was a crudely depicted Chicago peopled by fantastic
criminals: an ex-boxer, an ex-clergyman, a Japanese pickpocket

x Introduction

(played by Peter Lorre) and a policeman's mysterious widow
known as 'The Fly' or 'The Lady in Grey'.

Then with the 1930s came the talking film, notably the great
gangster movies associated with such actors as Humphrey
Bogart, James Cagney, Paul Muni, Bruce Cabot and Edward G.
Robinson. Brecht loved these, and it must have been their impact
which made *Ui* so much more vivid and dynamic a play than its
precursors (this is most visible perhaps in scenes 10 and 11, the
hotel and garage scenes). What is not certain is whether he knew
the stage or film version of *Winterset* (first produced in 1935), the
gangster play by Kurt Weill's new collaborator Maxwell
Anderson (whom he was subsequently to meet – and offend – in
New York), though clearly its application of verse forms to such
a theme would have intrigued him. Following *St Joan of the
Stockyards*, with its allusions to Goethe and Schiller and its use of
blank verse for the Chicago milieu, he himself had used a quasi-
Shakespearean structure and diction for *The Round Heads and the
Pointed Heads*, his anti-Nazi parable of the mid-thirties which he
set in an unconvincing Brechtian Ruritania. This conflict of
levels was originally intended not so much as a deliberate experi-
ment in incongruity (or 'alienation') but as a by-product of that
play's origins in an adaptation of *Measure for Measure*. But he
already saw something of the same bloodshed and violence in
Elizabethan high drama or Roman history (the setting of his
first tentative 'Ui' story, as outlined on pp. 119–20) as in Chicago
gang warfare or the Nazi street fighting of Hitler's rise to power.
To him there was nothing inappropriate in using the same 'grand
style' for all these things, and if it disconcerted the audience so
much the better.

Prior to his arrival in Scandinavia as a black-listed and dis-
enfranchised exile he had not tried to put the Nazis into a play,
though from 1931 on he was attacking them scathingly in such
poems as the 'Song of the SA man' and the parodistic 'Hitler
Chorales' – some at least of these works being written for left-
wing cabarets. In *The Round Heads and the Pointed Heads* the satire
was more oblique and may (so Gisela Bahr has suggested) have
been directed in the first place as much against Mussolini as
against the new German *Führer*; its somewhat distorted exposure
of Hitler's race policy was incorporated later. But during 1935,

probably as a result of his visit to Piscator in Moscow that spring, Brecht decided to write a series of quite realistic short sketches and playlets about life in Hitler's Third (would-be Thousand-Year) Reich. Grouped together under the title *Fear and Misery of the Third Reich* – and also known at various times and in various arrangements as 99%, *The Private Life of the Master Race* etc. – these concentrated entirely on ordinary middle- and low-level Germans rather than the strange mixture of orators, megalo-maniacs, pedagogues, third-rate intellectuals and brilliant military-bureaucratic technicians who ran the Reich from 1933 to 1945. Even before starting work on this wide but small-scale panorama Brecht had evidently realised that men like Hitler would need cruder and less objective treatment, and had seen the gangster movie as a possible model. With the ending of his short-lived realistic phase – which can be ascribed fairly exactly to the second half of 1938, when Brecht was working on *Galileo* and starting to chafe at its limitations – he was ready to get back to this idea and tackle the Nazi leaders head on.

In 1940 Brechts favourite film actor guyed Hitler and Mussolini in *The Great Dictator*, and if the war removed much of the daring and outrage of Chaplin's original conception it also made it a lot easier to get such satires shown. So Brecht too could now take Hitler and some of his chief associates (Göring, Goebbels, Von Papen, Röhm – though not Heinrich Himmler), and present them as protection-racket gangsters straight from the Al Capone-like milieu so brilliantly popularised by Warner Brothers and First National, while at the same time making them talk like characters out of Shakespeare. There was a double alienation at work here; first the events of Hitler's rise to power became transposed into the setting of (say) Dashiell Hammett's 'The Big Knockover', while secondly the underworld characters, with their talk of Brownings and the Bronx, moved into conscious parody of the high poetic drama: the Garden Scene from Goethe's *Faust* for instance in the rhymed couplets of scene 12, Mark Antony's speech in that with the old Shakespearian actor, the second scene of *Richard III* in Ui's wooing of the widow Dullfeet in scene 13. Both aspects of this operation presented new and intriguing problems to Brecht. On the one hand he had to establish the historical analogies without reducing the outward

and visible gangster story to a lifeless parable; which meant
striking a happy compromise (as it were) between *Scarface* and
Mein Kampf, and taking the lumbering epic theatre for an
unprecedentedly fast gallop over ground normally associated
with gun battles and car chases. On the other, the grand style of
the language had to go slumming, as in Ragg's speech of regret
for the fading gang leader –
    Yesterday's hero has been long forgotten
    His mug-shot gathers dust in ancient files
– culminating in the ironic explosion of 'Oh, lousy world!'. The
gratifying thing to him about this inconsistency of style and level
was that it was only brought out 'the inadequacy of [the Nazis']
masterful pose' but also, by its wilful manhandling of the blank
verse form, seemed to generate 'new formal material for a modern
verse with irregular rhythms, which could lead to great things'.

*   *   *

It must be remembered that Brecht was writing before the time
of the 'Final Solution', and many of the horrors which we now
associate with the Third Reich were still to come. Even such
historical events as are covered by the play had to be cut and
compressed, and the 'certain incidents in the recent past' which
loom up relentlessly at the end of each scene are far from giving
a complete picture of the period: in other words Hitler's triumph-
ant career from 1932, the last year of the Weimar Republic, up to
his unopposed takeover of Austria in 1938. It would be wrong to
attribute the gaps in this story primarily to shortcomings in
Brecht's own understanding of events, since it is generally
accepted (and borne out by the *Fear and Misery* sketches and such
poems as 'The Last Wish', written in 1935), that he made a
relentless effort to keep himself informed.

    Among his more substantial sources would probably have
been Konrad Heiden's pioneering life of Hitler, which appeared
in Switzerland in 1936, but above all the remarkably detailed and
well-illustrated 'Brown Books' compiled in Paris by the brilliant
Comintern propagandist Willi Muenzenberg and a whole team of
writers including Arthur Koestler and the clever but untrust-
worthy Otto Katz, former business manager of the Piscator
company with which Brecht had been associated in Berlin. The

first of these documents appeared as early as 1933, and made a
strong case against the Nazis – and particularly Göring – for
having themselves originated the Reichstag Fire. The second
dealt with the trial of the alleged Communist arsonists, the third
with the Nazi subversion and propaganda network in Austria and
other countries subsequently swallowed by Hitler. All three
contained liberal evidence of beatings and murders, already
naming Oranienburg, Buchenwald, Dachau and other now
notorious concentration camps.

What Brecht left out of his historical outline, as appended on
p. 101, was in the first place the role played by the Bulgarian
Communist Georgi Dimitrov, who with two of his compatriots
was among those framed in the show trial before the Leipzig
Supreme Court. This is surprising since Dimitrov became a great
left-wing hero as a result of his accusatory confrontation with
Göring; he was the principal figure of the second Brown Book.
Propaganda value apart, however, this episode was less important than the previous dismantling by Von Papen of the Socialist-
run Prussian provincial government and state apparatus: a
crucial step in smoothing the way for a right-wing dictatorship
which Brecht, once again, curiously omits. Yet neither of these
points seems to have disturbed his critics so much as his failure
to refer to Hitler's persecution of the Jews or to allow for any
kind of resistance by the German people. Not that the latter
omission should surprise anyone today, when a more realistic
view is taken of German support for the Nazis than prevailed
among their opponents at the time. But the decision to say
nothing whatever about the racial issue does seem a little odd
considering the big part which it had played five years before in
The Round Heads and the Pointed Heads. Possibly Brecht had come to
feel a little uneasy about the interpretation which he gave there;
possibly he just felt that he had had his say already. In any case the
gangster theme emerges as that much stronger and more
dynamic than the rather tangled story of the earlier play.

Otherwise the analogies set out in the outline are pretty well
correct. The Dock Aid scandal of the early scenes refers to the
Osthilfe, a form of state subsidy to the Junkers or East German
landowners – Brecht's Cauliflower Trust – one of whom, a baron
Von Oldenburg-Januschau, was a friend and neighbour of

President Hindenburg and had got up the subscription to buy him the former family estate of Neudeck – the country house of scene 4 – as a tribute for his eightieth birthday in 1929. For tax reasons this was put in the name of Colonel Oskar von Hindenburg, the old man's son and heir. Late in 1932, during the chancellorship of Oskar's slippery friend Franz von Papen – Clark of the Trust – the facts leaked out and threatened to upset Hindenburg's system of government by like-minded ex-officers and gentlemen, industrialists and landowners, by-passing the Reichstag thanks to his use of presidential decrees.

Hitler – Ui – whose party had been returned with 38% of the seats in the July Reichstag elections, was at that time still regarded by the president as a pretentious (non-commissioned) upstart unfit for high office; moreover by that autumn even his popular support showed symptoms of decline; – the occasion for Ragg's mock-lamentations. Papen however had legalised the SA, Hitler's brown-shirted private army under the leadership of Ernst Röhm – Roma – the former officer who was the party's 'Chief of Staff'. The gang was again free to threaten and brawl, while their leader started canvassing the industrialists and other influential conservatives on behalf of his precariously-financed party. That winter, with Papen and his successor Schleicher both unable to govern, Hitler's chancellorship appeared the only practical solution, so long as he and Göring could be contained within a cabinet of Papen and other orthodox nationalists. – So enter Ui in scene 5, with his 'Hi, Clark! Hi, Dogsborough! Hi, everybody!'. The upstart was on top.

Within a month of Hitler's appointment as chancellor on 30 January 1933 the now largely inoperative Reichstag building – the warehouse of scene 7 – had burned down: pretext for a wave of repression against the left wing, who were held responsible. The Communist view at that time was that the only one of the accused to be involved was the half-crazy unemployed Dutch youth Marinus van der Lubbe – Fish in scene 8 – who was caught on the premises, having supposedly been introduced by the real incendiaries, led by a particularly vile SA officer named Heines, through an underground passage from the house of Göring, the Reichstag president. This version is now generally accepted by historians, though a book by Fritz Tobias has argued that Van der Lubbe did the job entirely on his own. What is certain is that the suppression of all opposition and union activity within Germany dates from the fire; hence the Brechts' own departure on the following day, and hence also the symbolism of the Woman's speech of terror in scene 9a (though originally this was placed at the end of the play).

Next came the suppression of the quasi-revolutionary element within Hitler's own party – interpreted by Brecht, like Konrad Heiden before him, as the Nazi leader's attempt to legitimise himself as the declining Hindenburg's inevitable successor. On 30 June 1934 Hitler went to attend a conference of SA commanders called by Röhm at Bad Wiessee in Bavaria – the garage of scene 11 – taking Goebbels with him; they arrived with old party friends in an armoured column. Heines was shot out of hand, Röhm arrested and later shot in a prison cell; a total of 122 dead was later reported, while another 150 or so were executed under Goering's orders in Berlin and other, smaller, operations were simultaneously carried out elsewhere. Less than a month later, the Austrian chancellor Engelbert Dollfuss – 'a very small man' like Brecht's Ignatius Dullfeet – was also murdered by SS men as part of an unsuccessful Nazi coup against this Catholic-dominated country. He too had been a right-wing dictator with few humanitarian inhibitions, and although he was prepared to negotiate with the Nazis he would never do the same with the Left. For four years after his death the Austrians tried to play off Hitler against Mussolini before being finally absorbed by the former in the *Anschluss* (or reunification) of 1938, after which the seizure of Czechoslovakia and the German wartime conquests followed – the Washington, Milwaukee, Detroit and so on of Ui's closing speech. All the same, the play effectively follows events only up to 1935, the year of its original conception, and Brecht never wrote 'the utterly and universally unperformable' sequel which he felt the itch to start in April 1941 as soon as he had finished revising: '*Ui Part Two*, spain/munich/poland/france'. The real scale of Hitler's triumphs remains only as a prophetic threat.

*   *   *

Ui was not written for the desk drawer but, said Brecht, 'with the possibility of a production continually before my eyes; and that's the main reason why I so enjoyed it'. And yet only a few months after his arrival in California in July 1941 this possibility somehow slid out of reach, to be relegated to a remote corner of the back of his mind. What happened was that, having already failed to find any takers for Reyher's translation of the *Fear and Misery* scenes (under the title *The Devil's Sunday*), he almost at once proposed the new play to Piscator in New York with the suggestion that Oscar Homolka, then finding few satisfactory parts in Hollywood, should play the title part. Piscator and Hanns Eisler together persuaded H. R. Hays to make a rapid translation, arguing that they had got trade union support for a production. The translation was done by the end of September, and the script sent off to Louis Shaffer, director of Labor Stage. Shaffer however (in a letter quoted by James Lyon in *Brecht in America*) turned it down, saying

I gave the play to several people to read, and the opinion is, including my own, that it is not advisable to produce it.

This was of course before the United States entered the war, and in any case Hays was doubtful about giving the play to Piscator at all, and warned Brecht with some justification that his old colleague's first New York productions had been far from successful. However, as it turned out, the money was never raised; Hays lost interest when Brecht gave up answering his letters; and Brecht, though at some point he evidently resumed his revision of the play, soon put it away and seemingly forgot it. Only a cutting in his journal for January 1942 recalls his interest: this reproduced a cartoon captioned 'Murder Inc.', with Hitler as a gangster, smoking pistol in his hand, followed by his henchmen 'The Monk' and 'Benny the Fat'. 'See *Rise of Arturo Ui*!' says a handwritten note by Brecht, who also gummed the picture into his own copy of the script.

There the matter rested for the next ten years or so. There is no sign of any further interest in an English-language production, and the question of a German one still did not arise. For the only theatre which might have wished to put the play on in the war years was the Zurich Schauspielhaus, and for that company, with its large complement of refugee German actors, it would have been politically impossible: there is no evidence that Brecht ever bothered to submit it. Nor would he have trusted any postwar

German theatre company to stage a play on such a sensitive subject except under his own direction, even supposing that he had thought its satire appropriate to the immediate aftermath of defeat. So there was no question of bringing the play out again until after his return to Germany and the setting up of the Berliner Ensemble in 1949, and even then there were at least half-a-dozen other major plays which he wanted to stage himself and get properly established first. *Ui* was a problematic work, near the bottom of a very substantial pile. No part of it had been published in any form or discussed in the press, and not many people can even have known of its existence.

He first seems to have dug it out and shown it to a slightly wider circle in the second half of 1953: a time when the events of 17 June – the street riots in Berlin and the intervention of the Russian tanks – had forced him to take stock of his country with its Nazi survivals and Communist mistakes. That autumn he wrote the cycle of short, closely compressed 'Buckow Elegies', balancing half-veiled criticisms of the continuing Stalinism of the regime against uncomfortable glimpses of the Nazi heritage, seen in the shifty attitude of the village tradespeople, the military walk, the sudden upraised arm. It was in such a mood of renewed suspicion of his own people that he discussed the script with a group of writers along the lines suggested on pp. 109–10 and also (we don't quite know when) found himself explaining to his younger collaborators – dramaturgs and directors – why he did not think that it could yet be performed. His feeling, in effect, was that they were not mature enough to stand seeing Hitler mocked; the old sentiments were still too close to the surface. He told them that *Fear and Misery of the Third Reich* would have to be shown first: in other words that they could not stage *Ui* until they and their audience had taken the trouble to see exactly what they were mocking. One of the more painful pages of his journal shows him taking three of those collaborators out to Buckow and suddenly thinking that only ten years earlier any one of them, whatever their admiration for his work, would instantly have handed him over to the Gestapo. The passage is painful not because it is justified – which it surely was not – but because it shows the depth of Brecht's reservations about even the best of the German postwar generation.

It looks as if he was persuaded at least to prepare the play for publication, though in the event it was not to come out before he died. Instead it was first published by Peter Huchel in the memorial volume of the East German Academy's fat review *Sinn und Form*, along with the epilogue which Brecht had written for postwar audiences but not the second prologue (p. 106) nor his still incomplete notes. This volume appeared early in 1957, and around the same time five of the Ensemble's young assistant directors – Peter Palitzsch, Lothar Bellag, Käthe Rülicke, Carl Weber and the Pole Konrad Swinarski – staged scenes from *Fear and Misery of the Third Reich* against projections of historical photographs. The following year Palitzsch directed *Ui*'s world premiere in Stuttgart, West Germany, provoking his Ensemble colleague Manfred Wekwerth to the criticisms here reprinted on pp. 111–14: there was also a very interesting review by the leading West German critic Siegfried Melchinger which called the play 'a brilliant miscarriage' and took up the East German writer's point that the German people had been omitted, but then stood this argument on its head by complaining that Brecht had failed to show how a majority of them had voted Hitler into power; i.e. how Ui was not a mere creature of the trusts.

Four months later the Ensemble launched its own triumphal production – one of its outstanding box-office successes, and the first real demonstration of Brecht's continuing vitality after 1956 – with Palitzsch and Wekwerth as co-directors. This was staged in fairground style, with ruthless verve and brassy vulgarity, and it centred on one of the great acting performances of the past twenty-five years: Ekkehard Schall's clowning, acrobatic yet chillingly serious interpretation of the ghastly red-eyed, mackintoshed ham rhetorician Arturo Ui. Seen in Berlin, London and the Paris International Theatre Festival, it was one of the great proofs of Brecht's theatricality, for nobody reading the play, with its crude and obviously rather dated mockery of such (happily) defunct mass-murderers, could imagine that it would be so amusing, let alone so compelling to watch. And yet it caught the spectator up and propelled him along the curves and gradients of its rickety-looking structure, for all the world like a giant switchback. The experience was inspiring: theatres and television channels in one country after another tried to emulate it, as a succession of outstanding actors tackled the Ui role: Leonard Rossiter on stage and Nicol Williamson on television in Britain, Jean Vilar in Paris, John Bell in Sydney, Christopher Plummer and Al Pacino in the United States. Who would have thought the old man had so much blood in him?

*   *   *

Whether Brecht himself would have approved of the play's delayed success is another matter. Always liable to say the unexpected yet blindingly obvious, he might well have been disconcerted by the happy relief with which middle-class audiences everywhere fell on this apparent evidence that the monsters who forty years ago quite truly 'almost won the world' were only overgrown mobsters after all, something to laugh at and forget. Brecht had wanted to make his spectators feel uncomfortable, even as they noted the ridiculous disproportion between the stature of the Nazi leaders and the scale of their crimes; but certainly his play never achieved this in anything like the same measure as such inferior pieces of writing as *Holocaust* and *The Diary of Anne Frank*; moreover the parable might be expected to lose its sting progressively as the real-life events on which it reposes fade from the public mind. This is the dilemma facing any would-be director of *The Resistible Rise of Arturo Ui* today: he may be able to make a powerful theatrical event of it, but as he looks at Brecht's ingeniously self-justificatory notes on pp. 107–09 he is likely – if he has any kind of political conscience, to wonder whether it is nowadays possible to make it anything more.

The objects of Brecht's satire are dead, and neither their surviving followers nor their more ignorant imitators have been able to recreate anything resembling their reign. For whatever we may think of the reactionary regimes still to be found in the civilised world today no great technologically and administratively advanced country is now open to the unchecked rule of demagogues propelled by expansionist ambition and what the Nazis termed 'thinking with one's blood'. Modern right-wing or totalitarian governments are not in the same league as Hitler's Reich. But what does live on is the mindless violence of the hoodlum, which has now spread a great deal further within those

very societies, to haunt the football terraces, the film and
television screens and the imaginations of the elderly, sometimes
gratuitously, sometimes under the guise of legitimate social or
political grievance. It is this, not the specifically Nazi allusions,
that moves rapidly into the centre of the modern spectator's
awareness on seeing Brecht's play: not the threat of war nor even
the murder of political opponents but that same creeping low-
level brutality which we know to flourish under police regimes.
The surface parable, in short, has become closer to contemporary
life than the historical events for which it stands, and which are
steadily fading into a vague if abominable legend. The satire is on
the other foot, but it can still offer us a shock – the realisation that
our own society's violence might one day be parallelled by a
rebirth of Fascism on the grand scale.

So the alienating devices can change their function, as Brecht's
big plays come to convey a very different message from the one
they were planned to carry. *Galileo* becomes a defence of sceptical
human reason against imposed systems of thought; *Ui* a blasting
attack on the banal irrationality which can lead in certain circumstances to psychopathic government. Such works in other words
are continually shifting in relation to our times; they are still in
motion. In that sense they do indeed seem like the dispersed
fragments of some great explosion which took place about forty
years ago. But just at the moment they may be tending to come
together again.

THE EDITORS

The Resistible Rise of Arturo Ui
A parable play

Collaborator: M. STEFFIN

Translator: RALPH MANHEIM

Characters
THE ANNOUNCER
FLAKE
CARUTHER
BUTCHER   } *Businessmen, directors of the*
MULBERRY   *Cauliflower Trust*
CLARK
SHEET, *shipyard owner*
OLD DOGSBOROUGH
YOUNG DOGSBOROUGH
ARTURO UI, *gang leader*
ERNESTO ROMA, *his lieutenant*
EMANUELE GIRI, *gangster*
The florist GIUSEPPE GIVOLA, *gangster*
TED RAGG, *reporter on* The Star
DOCKDAISY

BOWL, *Sheet's chief accountant*
GOODWILL *and* GAFFLES, *members of the city council*
O'CASEY, *investigator*
AN ACTOR
HOOK, *wholesale vegetable dealer*
DEFENDANT FISH
THE DEFENCE COUNSEL
THE JUDGE
THE DOCTOR
THE PROSECUTOR
A WOMAN
YOUNG INNA, *Roma's familiar*
A LITTLE MAN
IGNATIUS DULLFEET
BETTY DULLFEET, *his wife*
Dogsborough's BUTLER

Bodyguards
Gunmen
Vegetable dealers of Chicago and Cicero
Reporters

Prologue

The Announcer steps before the curtain. Large notices are attached to the curtain: 'New developments in dock subsidy scandal' ... 'The true facts about Dogsborough's will and confession' ... 'Sensation at warehouse fire trial' ... 'Friends murder gangster Ernesto Roma' ... 'Ignatius Dullfeet blackmailed and murdered' ... 'Cicero taken over by gangsters'. Behind the curtain popular dance music.

THE ANNOUNCER:
Friends, tonight we're going to show –
Pipe down, you boys in the back row!
And, lady, your hat is in the way! –
Our great historical gangster play
Containing, for the first time, as you'll see
The truth about the scandalous dock subsidy.
Further we give you, for your betterment
Dogsborough's confession and testament.
Arturo Ui's rise while the stock market fell.
The notorious warehouse fire trial. What a sell!
The Dullfeet murder! Justice in a coma!
Gang warfare: the killing of Ernesto Roma!
All culminating in our stunning last tableau:
Gangsters take over the town of Cicero!
Brilliant performers will portray
The most eminent gangsters of our day.
You'll see some dead and some alive
Some by-gone and others that survive
Some born, some made – for instance, here we show

The good old honest Dogsborough!
Old Dogsborough steps before the curtain.
His hair is white, his heart is black.
Corrupt old man, you may step back.
Dogsborough bows and steps back.
The next exhibit on our list
Is Givola –
Givola has stepped before the curtain.
                    – the horticulturist.
His tongue's so slippery he'd know how
To sell you a billy-goat for a cow!
Short, says the proverb, are the legs of lies.
Look at his legs, just use your eyes.
Givola steps back limping.
Now to Emanuele Giri, the super-clown.
Come out, let's look you up and down!
Giri steps before the curtain and waves his hand at the audience.
One of the greatest killers ever known!
Okay, beat it!
Giri steps back with an angry look.
And lastly Public Enemy Number One
Arturo Ui. Now you'll see
The biggest gangster of all times
Whom heaven sent us for our crimes
Our weakness and stupidity!
Arturo Ui steps before the curtain and walks out along the footlights.
Doesn't he make you think of Richard the Third?
Has anybody ever heard
Of blood so ghoulishly and lavishly shed
Since wars were fought for roses white and red?
In view of this the management
Has spared no cost in its intent
To picture his spectacularly vile
Manoeuvres in the grandest style.
But everything you'll see tonight is true.

Nothing's invented, nothing's new
Or made to order just for you.
The gangster play that we present
Is known to our whole continent.
While the music swells and the sound of a machine-gun mingles with it, the Announcer retires with an air of bustling self-importance.

I

a

Financial district. Enter five businessmen, the directors of the Cauliflower Trust.

FLAKE: The times are bad.
CLARK: It looks as if Chicago
   The dear old girl, while on her way to market
   Had found her pocket torn and now she's starting
   To scrabble in the gutter for her pennies.
CARUTHER: Last Thursday Jones invited me and eighty
   More to a partridge dinner to be held
   This Monday. If we really went, we'd find
   No one to greet us but the auctioneer.
   This awful change from glut to destitution
   Has come more quickly than a maiden's blush.
   Vegetable fleets with produce for this city
   Still ply the lakes, but nowhere will you find
   A buyer.
BUTCHER: It's like darkness at high noon.
MULBERRY: Robber and Clive are being auctioned off.
CLARK: Wheeler – importing fruit since Noah's ark –
   Is bankrupt.
FLAKE: And Dick Havelock's garages
   Are liquidiating.
CARUTHER: Where is Sheet?
FLAKE: Too busy
   To come. He's dashing round from bank to bank.
CLARK: What? Sheet?
   Pause.

                            In other words, the cauliflower
Trade in this town is through.
BUTCHER: Come, gentlemen
Chin up! We're not dead yet.
MULBERRY: Call this a life?
BUTCHER: Why all the gloom? The produce business in
This town is basically sound. Good times
And bad, a city of four million needs
Fresh vegetables. Don't worry. We'll pull through.
CARUTHER: How are the stores and markets doing?
MULBERRY: Badly.
The customers buy half a head of cabbage
And that on credit.
CLARK: Our cauliflower's rotting.
FLAKE: Say, there's a fellow waiting in the lobby –
I only mention it because it's odd –
The name is Ui . . .
CLARK: The gangster?
FLAKE: Yes, in person.
He's smelled the stink and thinks he sees an opening.
Ernesto Roma, his lieutenant, says
They can convince shopkeepers it's not healthy
To handle other people's cauliflower.
He promises our turnover will double
Because, he says, the shopkeepers would rather
Buy cauliflower than coffins.
They laugh dejectedly.
CARUTHER: It's an outrage.
MULBERRY, *laughing uproariously*:
Bombs and machine guns! New conceptions of
Salesmanship! That's the ticket. Fresh young
Blood in the Cauliflower Trust. They heard
We had insomnia, so Mr Ui
Hastens to offer us his services.
Well, fellows, we'll just have to choose. It's him

Or the Salvation Army. Which one's soup
Do you prefer?
CLARK: I tend to think that Ui's
Is hotter.
CARUTHER: Throw him out!
MULBERRY: Politely though.
How do we know what straits we'll come to yet?
They laugh.
FLAKE, *to Butcher*:
What about Dogsborough and a city loan?
To the others.
Butcher and I cooked up a little scheme
To help us through our pesent money troubles.
I'll give it to you in a nutshell. Why
Shouldn't the city that takes in our taxes
Give us a loan, let's say, for docks that we
Would undertake to build, so vegetables
Can be brought in more cheaply? Dogsborough
Is influential. He could put it through.
Have you seen Dogsborough?
BUTCHER: Yes. He refuses
To touch it.
FLAKE: He refuses? Damn it, he's
The ward boss on the waterfront, and he
Won't help us!
CARUTHER: I've contributed for years
To his campaign fund.
MULBERRY: Hell, he used to run
Sheet's lunchroom. Before he took up politics
He got his bread and butter from the Trust.
That's rank ingratitude. It's just like I've been
Telling you, Flake. All loyalty is gone!
Money is short, but loyalty is shorter.
Cursing, they scurry from the sinking ship
Friend turns to foe, employee snubs his boss
And our old lunchroom operator

Who used to be all smiles is one cold shoulder.
Morals go overboard in times of crisis.

CARUTHER: I'd never have expected that of Dogsborough.

FLAKE: What's his excuse?

BUTCHER: He says our proposition
Is fishy.

FLAKE: What's fishy about building docks?
Think of the men we'd put to work.

BUTCHER: He says
He has his doubts about our building docks.

FLAKE: Outrageous!

BUTCHER: What? Not building?

FLAKE: No. His doubts.

CLARK: Then find somebody else to push the loan.

MULBERRY: Sure, there are other people.

BUTCHER: True enough.
But none like Dogsborough. No, take it easy.
The man is good.

CLARK: For what?

BUTCHER: He's honest. And
What's more, reputed to be honest.

FLAKE: Rot!

BUTCHER: He's got to think about his reputation.
That's obvious.

FLAKE: Who gives a damn? We need
A loan from City Hall. His reputation
Is his affair.

BUTCHER: You think so? I should say
It's ours. It takes an honest man to swing
A loan like this, a man they'd be ashamed
To ask for proofs and guarantees. And such
A man is Dogsborough. Old Dogsborough's
Our loan. All right, I'll tell you why. Because they
Believe in him. They may have stopped believing
In God, but not in Dogsborough. A hard-boiled
Broker, who takes a lawyer with him to

His lawyer's, wouldn't hesitate to put his
Last cent in Dogsborough's apron for safe keeping
If he should see it lying on the bar.
Two hundred pounds of honesty. In eighty
Winters he's shown no weakness. Such a man
Is worth his weight in gold – especially
To people with a scheme for building docks
And building kind of slowly.

FLAKE: Okay, Butcher
He's worth his weight in gold. The deal he vouches
For is tied up. The only trouble is:
He doesn't vouch for ours.

CLARK: Oh no, not he!
'The city treasury is not a grab bag!'

MULBERRY: And 'All for the city, the city for itself!'

CARUTHER: Disgusting. Not an ounce of humour.

MULBERRY: Once
His mind's made up, an earthquake wouldn't change it.
To him the city's not a place of wood
And stone, where people live with people
Struggling to feed themselves and pay the rent
But words on paper, something from the Bible.
The man has always gotten on my nerves.

CLARK: His heart was never with us. What does he care
For cauliflower and the trucking business?
Let every vegetable in the city rot
You think he'd lift a finger? No, for nineteen years
Or is it twenty, we've contributed
To his campaign fund. Well, in all that time
The only cauliflower he's ever seen
Was on his plate. What's more, he's never once
Set foot in a garage.

BUTCHER: That's right.

CLARK: The devil
Take him!

BUTCHER: Oh no! We'll take him.

FLAKE: But Clark says
It can't be done. The man has turned us down.
BUTCHER: That's so. But Clark has also told us why.
CLARK: The bastard doesn't know which way is up.
BUTCHER: Exactly. What's his trouble? Ignorance.
He hasn't got the faintest notion what
It's like to be in such a fix. The question
Is therefore how to put him in our skin.
In short, we've got to educate the man.
I've thought it over. Listen, here's my plan.
*A sign appears, recalling certain incidents in the recent past.**

b

Outside the produce exchange. Flake and Sheet in conversation.

SHEET: I've run from pillar to post. Pillar was out
Of town, and Post was sitting in the bathtub.
Old friends show nothing but their backs. A brother
Buys wilted shoes before he meets his brother
For fear his brother will touch him for a loan.
Old partners dread each other so they use
False names when meeting in a public place.
Our citizens are sewing up their pockets.
FLAKE: So what about my proposition?
SHEET: No. I
Won't sell. You want a five-course dinner for the
Price of the tip. And to be thanked for the tip
At that. You wouldn't like it if
I told you what I think of you.
FLAKE: Nobody
Will pay you any more.

* See the Chronological Table at the end of the play.

SHEET: And friends won't be
More generous than anybody else.
FLAKE: Money is tight these days.
SHEET: Especially
For those in need. And who can diagnose
A friend's need better than a friend?
FLAKE: You'll lose
Your shipyard either way.
SHEET: And that's not all
I'll lose. I've got a wife who's likely to
Walk out on me.
FLAKE: But if you sell . . .
SHEET: . . . she'll last another year. But what I'm curious
About is why you want my shipyard.
FLAKE: Hasn't
It crossed your mind that we – I mean the Trust –
Might want to help you?
SHEET: No, it never crossed
My mind. How stupid of me to suspect you
Of trying to grab my property, when you
Were only trying to help.
FLAKE: Such bitterness
Dear Sheet, won't save you from the hammer.
SHEET: At least, dear Flake, it doesn't help the hammer.
*Three men saunter past: Arturo Ui, the gangster, his lieutenant
Ernesto Roma, and a bodyguard. In passing, Ui stares at Flake
as though expecting to be spoken to, while, in leaving, Roma turns
his head and gives Flake an angry look.*
SHEET: Who's that?
FLAKE: Arturo Ui, the gangster . . . How
About it? Are you selling?
SHEET: He seemed eager
To speak to you.
FLAKE, *laughing angrily*: And so he is. He's been
Pursuing us with offers, wants to sell
Our cauliflower with his tommy guns.

　　The town is full of types like that right now
　　Corroding it like leprosy, devouring
　　A finger, then an arm and shoulder. No one
　　Knows where it comes from, but we all suspect
　　From deepest hell. Kidnapping, murder, threats
　　Extortion, blackmail, massacre:
　　'Hands up!' 'Your money or your life!' Outrageous!
　　It's got to be wiped out.
SHEET, *looking at him sharply*: And quickly. It's contagious.
FLAKE: Well, how about it? Are you selling?
SHEET, *stepping back and looking at him*:
　　No doubt about it: a resemblance to
　　Those three who just passed by. Not too pronounced
　　But somehow there, one senses more than sees it.
　　Under the water of a pond sometimes
　　You see a branch, all green and slimy. It
　　Could be a snake. But no, it's definitely
　　A branch. Or is it? That's how you resemble
　　Roma. Don't take offence. But when I looked
　　At him just now and then at you, it seemed
　　To me I'd noticed it before, in you
　　And others, without understanding. Say it
　　Again, Flake: 'How about it? Are you selling?'
　　Even your voice, I think . . . No, better say
　　'Hands up!' because that's what you really mean.
　　He puts up his hands.
　　All right, Flake, Take the shipyard!
　　Give me a kick or two in payment. Hold it!
　　I'll take the higher offer. Make it two.
FLAKE: You're crazy!
SHEET:　　　　　　　　　I only wish that that were true.

2

Back room in Dogsborough's restaurant. Dogsborough and his son are washing glasses. Enter Butcher and Flake.

DOGSBOROUGH: You didn't need to come. The answer is
No. Your proposition stinks of rotten fish.
YOUNG DOGSBOROUGH: My father turns it down.
BUTCHER: Forget it, then.
We ask you. You say no. So no it is.
DOGSBOROUGH: It's fishy. I know your kind of docks.
I wouldn't touch it.
YOUNG DOGSBOROUGH: My father wouldn't touch it.
BUTCHER: Good.
Forget it.
DOGSBOROUGH: You're on the wrong road, fellows.
The city treasury is not a grab bag
For everyone to dip his fingers into.
Anyway, damn it all, your business is
Perfectly sound.
BUTCHER: What did I tell you, Flake?
You fellows are too pessimistic.
DOGSBOROUGH: Pessimism
Is treason. You're only making trouble for
Yourselves. I see it this way: What do you
Fellows sell? Cauliflower. That's as good
As meat and bread. Man doesn't live by bread
And meat alone, he needs his green goods.
Suppose I served up sirloin without onions
Or mutton without beans. I'd never see
My customers again. Some people are
A little short right now. They hesitate
To buy a suit. But people have to eat.

They'll always have a dime for vegetables.
Chin up! If I were you, I wouldn't worry.
FLAKE: It does me good to hear you, Dogsborough.
It gives a fellow courage to go on.
BUTCHER: Dogsborough, it almost makes me laugh to find
You so staunchly confident about the future
Of cauliflower, because quite frankly we
Have come here for a purpose. No, don't worry.
Not what you think, that's dead and buried. Something
Pleasant, or so at least we hope. Old man
It's come to our attention that it's been
Exactly-twenty three years this June, since you –
Well known to us for having operated
The lunchroom in one of our establishments for
More than three decades – left us to devote
Your talents to the welfare of this city.
Yes, without you our town would not be what
It is today. Nor, like the city, would
The Trust have prospered as it has. I'm glad
To hear you call it sound, for yesterday
Moved by this festive occasion, we resolved
In token of our high esteem, as proof
That in our hearts we somehow still regard you
As one of us, to offer you the major share
Of stock in Sheet's shipyard for twenty thousand
Dollars, or less than half its value.
He lays the packet of stocks on the bar.
DOGSBOROUGH: I
Don't understand.
BUTCHER: Quite frankly, Dogsborough
The Cauliflower Trust is not reputed
For tenderness of heart, but yesterday
After we'd made our . . . well, our
Stupid request about the loan, and heard
Your answer, honest, incorruptible
Old Dogsborough to a hair, a few of us –

It's not an easy thing to say – were close
To tears. Yes, one man said – don't interrupt
Me, Flake, I won't say who – 'Good God'
He said, 'the man has saved us from ourselves.'
For some time none of us could speak. Then this
Suggestion popped up of its own accord.

DOGSBOROUGH:
I've heard you, friends. But what is there behind it?

BUTCHER: What should there be behind it? It's an offer.

FLAKE: And one that we are really pleased to make.
For here you stand behind your bar, a tower
Of strength, a sterling name, the model of
An upright citizen. We find you washing
Glasses, but you have cleansed our souls as well.
And yet you're poorer than your poorest guest.
It wrings our hearts.

DOGSBOROUGH: I don't know what to say.

BUTCHER: Don't say a word. Just take this little package.
An honest man can use it, don't you think?
By golly, it's not often that the gravy train
Travels the straight and narrow. Take your boy here:
I know a good name's better than a bank
Account, and yet I'm sure he won't despise it.
Just take the stuff and let us hope you won't
Read us the riot act for *this*!

DOGSBOROUGH: Sheet's shipyard!

FLAKE: Look, you can see it from right here.

DOGSBOROUGH, *at the window*:   I've seen it
For twenty years.

FLAKE: We thought of that.

DOGSBOROUGH: And what is
Sheet going to do?

FLAKE: He's moving into beer.

BUTCHER: Okay?

DOGSBOROUGH: I certainly appreciate

Your oldtime sentiments, but no one gives
Away a shipyard for a song.
FLAKE: There's something
In that. But now the loan has fallen through
Maybe the twenty thousand will come in handy.
BUTCHER: And possibly right now we're not too eager
To throw our stock upon the open market . . .
DOGSBOROUGH: That sounds more like it. Not a bad deal if
It's got no strings attached.
FLAKE: None whatsoever.
DOGSBOROUGH: The price you say is twenty thousand?
FLAKE: Is it
Too much?
DOGSBOROUGH: No. And imagine, it's the selfsame
Shipyard where years ago I opened my first lunchroom.
As long as there's no nigger in the woodpile . . .
You've really given up the loan?
FLAKE: Completely.
DOGSBOROUGH: I might consider it. Hey, look here, son
It's just the thing for you. I thought you fellows
Were down on me and here you make this offer.
You see, my boy, that honesty sometimes
Pays off. It's like you say: When I pass on
The youngster won't inherit much more than
My name, and these old eyes have seen what evil
Can spring from penury.
BUTCHER: We'll feel much better
If you accept. The ugly aftertaste
Left by our foolish proposition would be
Dispelled. In future we could benefit
By your advice. You'd show us how to ride
The slump by honest means, because our business
Would be your business, Dogsborough, because
You too would be a cauliflower man
And want the Cauliflower Trust to win.
Dogsborough takes his hand.

DOGSBOROUGH: Butcher and Flake, I'm in.
YOUNG DOGSBOROUGH: My father's in.
A sign appears.

3

Bookmaker's office on 122nd Street. Arturo Ui and his lieutenant Ernesto Roma, accompanied by bodyguards, are listening to the racing news on the radio. Next to Roma is Dockdaisy.

ROMA: I wish, Arturo, you could cure yourself
  Of this black melancholy, this inactive
  Dreaming. The whole town's talking.
UI, *bitterly*:   Talking? Who's talking?
  Nobody talks about me any more.
  This city's got no memory. Short-lived
  Is fame in such a place. Two months without
  A murder, and a man's forgotten.
  He whisks through the newspapers.
                    When
  The rod falls silent, silence strikes the press.
  Even when I deliver murders by the
  Dozen, I'm never sure they'll print them.
  It's not accomplishment that counts; it's
  Influence, which in turn depends on my
  Bank balance. Things have come to such a pass
  I sometimes think of chucking the whole business.
ROMA: The boys are chafing too from lack of cash.
  Morale is low. This inactivity's
  No good for them. A man with nothing but
  The ace of spades to shoot at goes to seed.
  I feel so sorry for those boys, Arturo
  I hate to show my face at headquarters. When
  They look at me, my 'Tomorrow we'll see action'

Sticks in my throat. Your vegetables idea was
So promising. Why don't we start right in?
UI: Not now. Not from the bottom. It's too soon.
ROMA: 'Too soon' is good. For four months now–
Remember? – since the Cauliflower Trust
Gave you the brush-off, you've been idly brooding.
Plans! Plans! Half-hearted feelers! That rebuff
Frizzled your spine. And then that little mishap –
Those cops at Harper's Bank – you've never gotten
Over it.
UI: But they fired!
ROMA: Only in
The air. That was illegal.
UI: Still too close
For me. I'd be in stir if they had plugged
My only witness. And that judge! Not two
Cent's worth of sympathy.
ROMA: The cops won't shoot
For grocery stores. They shoot for banks. Look here
Arturo, we'll start on Eleventh Street
Smash a few windows, wreck the furniture
Pour kerosene on the veg. And then we work
Our way to Seventh. Two or three days later
Giri, a posy in his buttonhole
Drops in and offers our protection for
A suitable percentage on their sales.
UI: No. First I need protection for myself
From cops and judges. Then I'll start to think
About protecting other people. We've
Got to start from the top.
Gloomily:
                          Until I've put the
Judge in my pocket by slipping something
Of mine in his, the law's against me. I
Can't even rob a bank without some two-bit cop
Shooting me dead.

ROMA: You're right. Our only hope is
   Givola's plan. He's got a nose for smells
   And if he says the Cauliflower Trust
   Smells promisingly rotten, I believe
   There's something in it. And there *was* some talk
   When, as they say, on Dogsborough's commendation
   The city made that loan. Since then I've heard
   Rumours about some docks that aren't being built
   But ought to be. Yet on the other hand
   Dogsborough recommended it. Why should
   That do-good peg for fishy business? Here comes
   Ragg of the 'Star'. If anybody knows
   About such things, it's him. Hi Ted.
RAGG, *slightly drunk*:   Hi, boys!
   Hi, Roma! Hi, Arturo! How are things in
   Capua?
UI: What's he saying?
RAGG: Oh, nothing much.
   That was a one-horse town where long ago
   An army went to pot from idleness
   And easy living.
UI: Go to hell!
ROMA, *to Ragg*:   No fighting.
   Tell us about that loan the Cauliflower
   Trust wangled.
RAGG: What do you care? Say! Could you
   Be going into vegetables? I've got it!
   You're angling for a loan yourselves. See Dogsborough.
   He'll put it through.
   Imitating the old man:
                    'Can we allow a business
   Basically sound but momentarily
   Threatened with blight, to perish?' Not an eye
   At City Hall but fills with tears. Deep feeling
   For cauliflower shakes the council members
   As though it were a portion of themselves.

Too bad, Arturo, guns call forth no tears.
The other customers laugh.
ROMA: Don't bug him, Ted. He's out of sorts.
RAGG: I shouldn't
Wonder. I hear that Givola has been
To see Capone for a job.
DOCKDAISY: You liar!
You leave Giuseppe out of this!
RAGG: Hi, Dockdaisy!
Still got your place in Shorty Givola's harem?
Introducing her:
Fourth super in the harem of the third
Lieutenant of a –
Points to Ui.
                         – fast declining star
Of second magnitude! Oh, bitter fate!
DOCKDAISY: Somebody shut the rotten bastard up!
RAGG: Posterity plaits no laurels for the gangster!
New heroes captivate the fickle crowd.
Yesterday's hero has been long forgotten
His mug-shot gathers dust in ancient files.
'Don't you remember, folks, the wounds I gave you?' –
'When?' – 'Once upon a time.' – 'Those wounds have
Turned to scars long since.' Alas, the finest scars
Get lost with those who bear them. 'Can it be
That in a world where good deeds go unnoticed
No monument remains to evil ones?' –
'Yes, so it is.' – 'Oh, lousy world!'
UI, *bellows:*   Shut
Him up!
The bodyguards approach Ragg.
RAGG, *turning pale:* Be careful, Ui. Don't insult
The press.
The other customers have risen to their feet in alarm.
ROMA: You'd better beat it, Ted. You've said
Too much already.

RAGG, *backing out, now very much afraid*:
     See you later, boys.
The room empties quickly.
ROMA: Your nerves are shot, Arturo.
UI: Those bastards
 Treat me like dirt.
ROMA: Because of your long silence.
 No other reason.
UI, *gloomily*:   Say, what's keeping Giri
 And that accountant from the Cauliflower
 Trust?
ROMA: They were due at three.
UI: And Givola?
 What's this I hear about him seeing Capone?
ROMA: Nothing at all. He's in his flower shop
 Minding his business, and Capone comes in
 To buy some wreaths.
UI: Some wreaths? For who?
ROMA: Not us.
UI: I'm not so sure.
ROMA: You're seeing things too black.
 Nobody's interested in us.
UI: Exactly.
 They've more respect for dirt. Take Givola.
 One setback and he blows. By God
 I'll settle his account when things look up.
ROMA: Giri!
Enter Emanuele Giri with a rundown individual, Bowl.
GIRI: I've got him, boss.
ROMA, *to Bowl*:   They tell me you
 Are Sheet's accountant at the Cauliflower
 Trust.
BOWL: Was. Until last week that bastard . . .
GIRI: He hates the very smell of cauliflower.
BOWL: Dogsborough . . .
UI, *quickly*:   Dogsborough! What about him?

ROMA: What have you got to do with Dogsborough?
GIRI: That's why I brought him.
BOWL: Dogsborough
Fired me.
ROMA: He fired you? From Sheet's shipyard?
BOWL: No, from his own. He took it over on
September first.
ROMA: What's that?
GIRI: Sheet's shipyard
Belongs to Dogsborough. Bowl here was present
When Butcher of the Cauliflower Trust
Handed him fifty-one percent of the stock.
UI: So what?
BOWL: So what? It's scandalous . . .
GIRI   Don't you
Get it, boss?
BOWL: . . . Dogsborough sponsoring that
Loan to the Cauliflower Trust . . .
GIRI: . . . when he
Himself was secretly a member of
The Cauliflower Trust.
UI, *who is beginning to see the light*:
                        Say, that's corrupt.
By God the old man hasn't kept his nose
Too clean.
BOWL: The loan was to the Cauliflower
Trust, but they did it through the shipyard. Through
Me. And I signed for Dogsborough. Not for Sheet
As people thought.
GIRI: By golly, it's a killer.
Old Dogsborough. The trusty and reliable
Signboard. So honest. So responsible!
Whose handshake was an honour and a pledge!
The staunch and incorruptible old man!
BOWL: I'll make the bastard pay. Can you imagine?
Firing me for embezzlement when he himself . . .

ROMA: Cool it! You're not the only one whose blood
Boils at such abject villainy. What do
You say, Arturo?
UI, *referring to Bowl*:
                    Will he testify?
GIRI: He'll testify.
UI, *grandly getting ready to leave*:
                    Keep an eye on him, boys. Let's go
Roma. I smell an opening.
*He goes out quickly, followed by Ernesto Roma and the body-
guards.*
GIRI, *slaps Bowl on the back*: Bowl, I
Believe you've set a wheel in motion, which . . .
BOWL: I hope you'll pay me back for any loss . . .
GIRI: Don't worry about that. I know the boss.
A sign appears.

4

Dogsborough's country house. Dogsborough and his son.

DOGSBOROUGH: I should never have accepted this estate.
Taking that package as a kind of gift was
Beyond reproach.
YOUNG DOGSBOROUGH: Of course it was.
DOGSBOROUGH: And sponsoring
That loan, when I discovered to my own
Detriment that a thriving line of business
Was languishing for lack of funds, was hardly
Dishonest. But when, confident the shipyard
Would yield a handsome profit, I accepted
This house before I moved the loan, so secretly
Acting in my own interest – that was wrong.
YOUNG DOGSBOROUGH: Yes, father.

DOGSBOROUGH: That was faulty judgment
Or might be so regarded. Yes, my boy
I should never have accepted this estate.
YOUNG DOGSBOROUGH: No.
DOGSBOROUGH: We've stepped into a trap.
YOUNG DOGSBOROUGH: Yes, father.
DOGSBOROUGH: That
Package of stocks was like the salty titbit
They serve free gratis at the bar to make
The customer, appeasing his cheap hunger
Work up a raging thirst.
Pause.
                              That inquiry
At City Hall about the docks, has got
Me down. The loan's used up. Clark helped
Himself; so did Caruther, Flake and Butcher
And so, I'm sad to say, did I. And no
Cement's been bought yet, not a pound! The one
Good thing is this: at Sheet's request I kept
The deal a secret; no one knows of my
Connection with the shipyard.
A BUTLER *enters*:   Telephone
Sir, Mr Butcher of the Cauliflower
Trust.
DOGSBOROUGH: Take it, son.
*Young Dogsborough goes out with the Butler. Church bells are
heard in the distance.*
DOGSBOROUGH   Now what can Butcher want?
Looking out of the window.
Those poplars are what tempted me to take
The place. The poplars and the lake down there, like
Silver before it's minted into dollars.
And air that's free of beer fumes. The fir trees
Are good to look at too, especially
The tops. Grey-green and dusty. And the trunks –

Their colour calls to mind the leathers we used to wrap
   around
The taps when drawing beer. It was the poplars, though
That turned the trick. Ah yes, the poplars.
It's Sunday. Hm. The bells would sound so peaceful
If the world were not so full of wickedness.
But what can Butcher want on Sunday?
I never should have . . .
YOUNG DOGSBOROUGH, *returning*: Father, Butcher says
Last night the City Council voted to
Investigate the Cauliflower Trust's
Projected docks. Father, what's wrong?
DOGSBOROUGH: My smelling salts!
YOUNG DOGSBOROUGH, *gives them to him*:
   Here.
DOGSBOROUGH: What does Butcher want?
YOUNG DOGSBOROUGH: He wants to come here.
DOGSBOROUGH: Here? I refuse to see him. I'm not well.
My heart.
He stands up. Grandly:
I haven't anything to do
With this affair. For sixty years I've trodden
The narrow path, as everybody knows.
They can't involve me in their schemes.
YOUNG DOGSBOROUGH: No, father.
Do you feel better now?
THE BUTLER *enters*:   A Mr Ui
Desires to see you, sir.
DOGSBOROUGH: The gangster!
THE BUTLER: Yes
I've seen his picture in the papers. Says he
Was sent by Mr Clark of the Cauliflower
Trust.
DOGSBOROUGH:
   Throw him out! Who sent him? Clark? Good God!
   Is he threatening me with gangsters now? I'll . . . .

Enter Arturo Ui and Ernesto Roma.

UI: Mr
  Dogsborough.
DOGSBOROUGH: Get out!
ROMA: I wouldn't be in such
  A hurry, friend. It's Sunday. Take it easy.
DOGSBOROUGH: Get out, I said!
YOUNG DOGSBOROUGH: My father says: Get out!
ROMA: Saying it twice won't make it any smarter.
UI, *unruffled*:
  Mr Dogsborough.
DOGSBOROUGH: Where are the servants? Call the
  Police.
ROMA: I wouldn't leave the room if I
  Were you, son. In the hallway you might run
  Into some boys who wouldn't understand.
DOGSBOROUGH: Ho! Violence!
ROMA: I wouldn't call it that.
  Only a little emphasis perhaps.
UI: Mr Dogsborough. I am well aware that you
  Don't know me, or even worse, you know me but
  Only from hearsay. Mr Dogsborough
  I have been very much maligned, my image
  Blackened by envy, my intentions disfigured
  By baseness. When some fourteen years ago
  Yours truly, then a modest, unemployed
  Son of the Bronx, appeared within the gates
  Of this your city to launch a new career
  Which, I may say, has not been utterly
  Inglorious, my only followers
  Were seven youngsters, penniless like myself
  But brave and like myself determined
  To cut their chunk of meat from every cow
  The Lord created. I've got thirty now
  And will have more. But now you're wondering: What
  Does Arturo Ui want of me? Not much. Just this.

What irks me is to be misunderstood
To be regarded as a fly-by-night
Adventurer and heaven knows what else.
Clears his throat.
Especially by the police, for I
Esteem them and I'd welcome their esteem.
And so I've come to ask you – and believe me
Asking's not easy for my kind of man –
To put a word in for me with the precinct
When necessary.
DOGSBOROUGH, *incredulously*:
                    Vouch for you, you mean?
UI: If necessary. That depends on whether
We strike a friendly understanding with
The vegetable dealers.
DOGSBOROUGH: What is your
Connection with the vegetable trade?
UI: That's what I'm coming to. The vegetable
Trade needs protection. By force if necessary.
And I'm determined to supply it.
DOGSBOROUGH: No
One's theatening it as far as I can see.
UI: Maybe not. Not yet. But I see further. And
I ask you: How long with our corrupt police
Force will the vegetable dealer be allowed
To sell his vegetables in peace? A ruthless
Hand may destroy his little shop tomorrow
And make off with his cash-box. Would he not
Prefer at little cost to arm himself
Before the trouble starts, with powerful protection?
DOGSBOROUGH: I doubt it.
UI: That would mean he doesn't know
What's good for him. Quite possible. The small
Vegetable dealer, honest but short-sighted
Hard-working but too often unaware
Of his best interest, needs strong leadership.

Moreover, toward the Cauliflower Trust
That gave him everything he has, he feels
No sense of responsibility. That's where I
Come in again. The Cauliflower Trust
Must likewise be protected. Down with the welshers!
Pay up, say I, or close your shop! The weak
Will perish. Let them, that's the law of nature.
In short, the Trust requires my services.
DOGSBOROUGH: But what's the Cauliflower Trust to me?
Why come to me with this amazing plan?
UI: We'll get to that. I'll tell you what you need.
The Cauliflower Trust needs muscle, thirty
Determined men under my leadership.
DOGSBOROUGH:
Whether the Trust would want to change its typewriters
For tommy-guns I have no way of knowing.
You see, I'm not connected with the Trust.
UI: We'll get to that. You say: With thirty men
Armed to the teeth, at home on our premises
How do we know that we ourselves are safe?
The answer's very simple. He who holds
The purse strings holds the power. And it's you
Who hand out the pay envelopes. How could
I turn against you even if I wanted
Even without the high esteem I bear you?
For what do I amount to? What
Following have I got? A handful. And some
Are dropping out. Right now it's twenty. Or less.
Without your help I'm finished. It's your duty
Your human duty to protect me from
My enemies, and (I may as well be frank)
My followers too! The work of fourteen years
Hangs in the balance! I appeal to you
As man to man.
DOGSBOROUGH: As man to man I'll tell
You what I'll do. I'm calling the police.

UI: What? The police?

DOGSBOROUGH: Exactly, the police!

UI: Am I to understand that you refuse
To help me as a man?
Bellows.

            Then I demand
It of you as a criminal. Because
That's what you are. I'm going to expose you.
I've got the proofs. There's going to be a scandal
About some docks. And you're mixed up in it. Sheet's
Shipyard – that's you. I'm warning you! Don't
Push me too far! They've voted to investigate.

DOGSBOROUGH, *very pale*:
They never will. They can't. My friends . . .

UI: You haven't got any. You had some yesterday.
Today you haven't got a single friend
Tomorrow you'll have nothing but enemies.
If anybody can rescue you, it's me
Arturo Ui! Me! Me!

DOGSBOROUGH: Nobody's going to
Investigate. My hair is white.

UI: But nothing else
Is white about you, Dogsborough.
Tries to seize his hand.
Think, man! It's now or never. Let me save you!
One word from you and any bastard who
Touches a hair of yon white head, I'll drill him.
Dogsborough, help me now. I beg you. Once.
Just once! Oh, say the word, or I shall never
Be able to face my boys again.
He weeps.

DOGSBOROUGH: Never!
I'd sooner die than get mixed up with you.

UI: I'm washed up and I know it. Forty
And still a nobody. You've got to help me.

DOGSBOROUGH: Never.

UI: I'm warning you. I'll crush you.
DOGSBOROUGH: Never
Never while I draw breath will you get away with
Your green goods racket.
UI, *with dignity*:   Mr Dogsborough
I'm only forty. You are eighty. With God's
Help I'll outlast you. And one thing I know:
I'll break into the green goods business yet.
DOGSBOROUGH: Never!
UI: Come, Roma. Let's get out of here.
He makes a formal bow and leaves the room with Ernesto Roma.
DOGSBOROUGH: Air! Give me air. Oh, what a mug!
Oh, what a mug! I should never have accepted
This estate. But they won't dare. I'm sunk
If they investigate, but they won't dare.
THE BUTLER *enters*: Goodwill and Gaffles of the city
   council.
Enter Goodwill and Gaffles.
GOODWILL: Hello, Dogsborough.
DOGSBOROUGH: Hello, Goodwill and Gaffles.
Anything new?
GOODWILL: Plenty, and not so good, I fear.
But wasn't that Arturo Ui who
Just passed us in the hall?
DOGSBOROUGH, *with a forced laugh*: Himself in person.
Hardly an ornament to a country home.
GOODWILL: No.
Hardly an ornament. It's no good wind
That brings us. It's that loan we made the Trust
To build their docks with.
DOGSBOROUGH, *stiffly*:   What about the loan?
GAFFLES: Well, certain council members said – don't get
Upset – the thing looked kind of fishy.
DOGSBOROUGH: Fishy.
GOODWILL: Don't worry The majority flew off
The handle. Fishy! We almost came to blows.

GAFFLES: Dogsborough's contracts fishy! they shouted.
 What
 About the Bible? Is that fishy too?
 It almost turned to an ovation for you
 Dogsborough. When your friends demanded an
 Investigation, some, infected with
 Our confidence, withdrew their motion and
 Wanted to shelve the whole affair. But the
 Majority, resolved to clear your name
 Of every vestige of suspicion, shouted:
 Dogsborough's more than a name. It stands for more
   than
 A man. It's an institution! In an uproar
 They voted the investigation.
DOGSBOROUGH: The
 Investigation.
GOODWILL: O'Casey is in charge.
 The cauliflower people merely say
 The loan was made directly to Sheet's shipyard.
 The contracts with the builders were to be
 Negotiated by Sheet's shipyard.
DOGSBOROUGH: By Sheet's shipyard.
GOODWILL: The best would be for you to send a man
 Of flawless reputation and impartiality
 Someone you trust, to throw some light on this
 Unholy rat's nest.
DOGSBOROUGH: So I will.
GAFFLES: All right
 That settles it. And now suppose you show us
 This famous country house of yours. We'll want
 To tell our friends about it.
DOGSBOROUGH: Very well.
GOODWILL:
 What blessed peace! And church bells! All one can
 Wish for.

GAFFLES, *laughing*:
     No docks in sight.
DOGSBOROUGH: I'll send a man.
     They go out slowly.
     A sign appears.

5

*City Hall. Butcher, Flake, Clark, Mulberry, Caruther. Across
from them Dogsborough, who is as white as a sheet, O'Casey,
Gaffles and Goodwill. Reporters.*

BUTCHER, *in an undertone*:
     He's late.
MULBERRY: He's bringing Sheet. Quite possibly
     They haven't come to an agreement. I
     Believe they've been discussing it all night.
     Sheet *has* to say the shipyard still belongs
     To him.
CARUTHER: It's asking quite a lot of Sheet
     To come here just to tell us *he's* the scoundrel.
FLAKE: He'll never come.
CLARK: He's got to.
FLAKE: Why should he
     Ask to be sent to prison for five years?
CLARK: It's quite a pile of dough. And Mabel Sheet
     Needs luxury. He's still head over heels
     In love with Mabel. He'll play ball all right.
     And anyway he'll never serve his term.
     Old Dogsborough will see to that.
     The shouts of newsboys are heard. A reporter brings in a paper.
GAFFLES: Sheet's been found dead. In his hotel. A ticket
     To San Francisco in his pocket.

BUTCHER: Sheet
   Dead?
O'CASEY, *reading*:
   Murdered.
MULBERRY: My God!
FLAKE, *in an undertone*:   He didn't come.
GAFFLES: What is it, Dogsborough?
DOGSBOROUGH, *speaking with difficulty*:
                        Nothing. It'll pass.
O'CASEY: Sheet's death . . .
CLARK: Poor Sheet. His unexpected death
   Would seem to puncture your investigation . . .
O'CASEY: Of course the unexpected often looks
   As if it were expected. Some indeed
   Expect the unexpected. Such is life.
   This leaves me in a pretty pickle and
   I hope you won't refer me and my questions
   To Sheet; for Sheet, according to this paper
   Has been most silent since last night.
MULBERRY: Your questions?
   You know the loan was given to the shipyard
   Don't you?
O'CASEY: Correct. But there remains a question:
   Who is the shipyard?
FLAKE, *under his breath*: Funny question! He's
   Got something up his sleeve.
CLARK, *likewise*:   I wonder what.
O'CASEY:
   Something wrong, Dogsborough? Could it be the air?
   To the others.
   I only mean: some people may be thinking
   That several shovelsful of earth are not
   Enough to load on Sheet, and certain muck
   Might just as well be added. I suspect . . .
CLARK: Maybe you'd better not suspect too much

O'Casey. Ever hear of slander? We've
Got laws agaist it.
MULBERRY: What's the point of these
Insinuations? Dogsborough, they tell me
Has picked a man to clear this business up.
Let's wait until he comes.
O'CASEY: He's late. And when
He comes, I hope Sheet's not the only thing
He'll talk about.
FLAKE: We hope he'll tell the truth
No more no less.
O'CASEY: You mean the man is honest?
That suits me fine. Since Sheet was still alive
Last night, the whole thing should be clear. I only –
To Dogsborough.
– Hope that you've chosen a good man.
CLARK, *cuttingly*:   You'll have
To take him as he is. Ah, here he comes.
Enter Arturo Ui and Ernesto Roma with bodyguards.
UI: Hi, Clark! Hi, Dogsborough! Hi, everybody!
CLARK: Hi, Ui.
UI: Well, it seems you've got some questions.
O'CASEY, *to Dogsborough*:
Is this your man?
CLARK: That's right, Not good enough?
GOODWILL: Dogsborough, can you be . . . ?
Commotion among the reporters.
O'CASEY: Quiet over there!
A REPORTER: It's Ui!
*Laughter. O'Casey bangs his gavel for order. Then he musters
the bodyguards.*
O'CASEY: Who are these men?
UI: Friends.
O'CASEY, *to Roma*:   And who
Are you?
UI: Ernesto Roma, my accountant.

GAFFLES: Hold it! Can you be serious, Dogsborough?
Dogsborough is silent.
O'CASEY: Mr
Ui, we gather from Mr Dogsborough's
Eloquent silence that you have his confidence
And desire ours. Well then. Where are the contracts?
UI: What contracts?
CLARK, *seeing that O'Casey is looking at Goodwill*:
                    The contracts that the shipyard no doubt
Signed with the builders with a view to enlarging
Its dock facilities.
UI: I never heard
Of any contracts.
O'CASEY: Really?
CLARK: Do you mean
There are no contracts?
O'CASEY, *quickly*:   Did you talk with Sheet?
UI, *shaking his head*:
No.
CLARK: Oh. You didn't talk with Sheet?
UI, *angrily*:   If any-
One says I talked with Sheet, that man's a liar.
O'CASEY: Ui, I thought that Mr Dogsborough
Had asked you to look into this affair?
UI: I have looked into it.
O'CASEY: And have your studies
Borne fruit?
UI: They have. It wasn't easy to
Lay bare the truth. And it's not a pleasant truth.
When Mr Dogsborough, in the interest of
This city, asked me to investigate
Where certain city funds, the hard-earned savings
Of taxpayers like you and me, entrusted
To a certain shipyard in this city, had gone to
I soon discovered to my consternation
That they had been embezzled. That's Point One.

Point Two is who embezzled them. All right
I'll answer that one too. The guilty party
Much as it pains me is . . .

o'casey: Well, who is it?

ui: Sheet.

o'casey: Oh, Sheet! The silent Sheet you didn't talk to!

ui: Why look at me like that? The guilty party
Is Sheet.

clark: Sheet's dead. Didn't you know?

ui: What, dead?
I was in Cicero last night. That's why
I haven't heard. And Roma here was with me.
Pause.

roma: That's mighty funny. Do you think it's mere
Coincidence that . . .

ui: Gentlemen, it's not
An accident. Sheet's suicide was plainly
The consequence of Sheet's embezzlement.
It's monstrous!

o'casey: Except it wasn't suicide.

ui: What then? Of course Ernesto here and I
Were in Cicero last night. We wouldn't know.
But this we know beyond a doubt: that Sheet
Apparently an honest businessman
Was just a gangster.

o'casey: Ui, I get your drift.
You can't find words too damaging for Sheet
After the damage he incurred last night.
Well, Dogsborough, let's get to you.

dogsborough: To me?

butcher, *cuttingly*:
What about Dogsborough?

o'casey: As I understand Mr
Ui – and I believe I understand
Him very well – there was a shipyard which
Borrowed some money which has disappeared.

But now the question rises: Who is this
Shipyard? It's Sheet, you say. But what's a name?
What interests us right now is not its name
But whom it actually belonged to. Did it
Belong to Sheet? Unquestionably Sheet
Could tell us. But Sheet has buttoned up
About his property since Ui spent
The night in Cicero. But could it be
That when this swindle was put over someone
Else was the owner? What is your opinion
Dogsborough?

DOGSBOROUGH: Me?

O'CASEY: Yes, could it be that you
Were sitting in Sheet's office when a contract
Was . . . well, suppose we say, not being drawn up?

GOODWILL: O'Casey!

GAFFLES, *to O'Casey*:

Dogsborough? You're crazy!

DOGSBOROUGH: I . . .

O'CASEY: And earlier, at City Hall, when you
Told us how hard a time the cauliflower
People were having and how badly they
Needed a loan – could that have been the voice
Of personal involvement?

BUTCHER: Have you no shame?
The man's unwell.

CARUTHER: Consider his great age!

FLAKE:
His snow-white hair confounds your low suspicions.

ROMA: Where are your proofs?

O'CASEY: The proofs are . . .

UI   Quiet, please!
Let's have a little quiet, friends.
Say something, Dogsborough!

A BODYGUARD, *suddenly roars*: The chief wants quiet!
Quiet!

Sudden silence.

UI: If I may say what moves me in
This hour and at this shameful sight – a white-
Haired man insulted while his friends look on
In silence – it is this. I trust you, Mr
Dogsborough. And I ask: Is this the face
Of guilt? Is this the eye of one who follows
Devious ways? Can you no longer
Distinguish white from black? A pretty pass
If things have come to such a pass!

CLARK: A man of
Untarnished reputation is accused
Of bribery.

O'CASEY: And more: of fraud. For I
Contend that this unholy shipyard, so
Maligned when Sheet was thought to be the owner
Belonged to Dogsborough at the time the loan
Went through.

MULBERRY: A filthy lie!

CARUTHER: I'll stake my head
For Dogsborough. Summon the population!
I challenge you to find one man to doubt him.

A REPORTER, *to another who has come in*:
Dogsborough's under suspicion.

THE OTHER REPORTER: Dogsborough?
Why not Abe Lincoln?

MULBERRY *and* FLAKE: Witnesses!

O'CASEY: Oh
It's witnesses you want? Hey, Smith, where *is*
Our witness? Is he here? I see he is.
*One of his men has stepped into the doorway and made a sign.
All look toward the door. Short pause. Then a burst of shots
and noise are heard. Tumult. The reporters run out.*

THE REPORTERS: It's outside. A machine-gun. – What's
your witness's name, O'Casey? – Bad business. – Hi, Ui!

o'CASEY, *going to the door*: Bowl! *Shouts out the door.* Come
   on in!
THE MEN OF THE CAULIFLOWER TRUST: What's going
   on? – Somebody's been shot – On the stairs – God damn it!
BUTCHER, *to Ui*:
   More monkey business? Ui, it's all over
   Between us if . . .
UI: Yes?
o'CASEY: Bring him in!
Policemen carry in a corpse.
o'CASEY: It's Bowl. My witness, gentlemen, I fear
   Is not in a fit state for questioning.
   *He goes out quickly. The policemen have set down Bowl's body
   in a corner.*
DOGSBOROUGH:
   For God's sake, Gaffles, get me out of here!
   Without answering Gaffles goes out past him.
UI, *going toward Dogsborough with outstretched hand*:
   Congratulations, Dogsborough. Don't doubt
   One way or another, I'll get things straightened out.
   A sign appears.

6

*Hotel Mammoth. Ui's suite. Two bodyguards lead a ragged actor
to Ui. In the background Givola.*

FIRST BODYGUARD: It's an actor, boss. Unarmed.
SECOND BODYGUARD: He can't afford a rod. He was able to
   get tight because they pay him to declaim in the saloons
   when they're tight. But I'm told that he's good. He's one
   of them classical guys.
UI: Okay. Here's the problem. I've been given to understand
   that my pronunciation leaves something to be desired. It

looks like I'm going to have to say a word or two on certain occasions, especially when I get into politics, so I've decided to take lessons. The gestures too.

THE ACTOR: Very well.

UI: Get the mirror.

A bodyguard comes front stage with a large standing mirror.

UI: First the walk. How do you guys walk in the theatre or the opera?

THE ACTOR: I see what you mean. The grand style. Julius Caesar, Hamlet, Romeo – that's Shakespeare. Mr Ui, you've come to the right man. Old Mahonney can teach you the classical manner in ten minutes. Gentlemen, you see before you a tragic figure. Ruined by Shakespeare. An English poet. If it weren't for Shakespeare, I could be on Broadway right now. The tragedy of a character. 'Don't play Shakespeare when you're playing Ibsen, Mahonney! Look at the calendar! This is 1912, sir!' – 'Art knows no calendar, sir!' say I. 'And art is my life.' Alas.

GIVOLA: I think you've got the wrong guy, boss. He's out of date.

UI: We'll see about that. Walk around like they do in this Shakespeare.

The actor walks around.

UI: Good!

GIVOLA: You can't walk like that in front of cauliflower men. It ain't natural.

UI: What do you mean it ain't natural? Nobody's natural in this day and age. When I walk I want people to know I'm walking.

He copies the actor's gait.

THE ACTOR: Head back. *Ui throws his head back.* The foot touches the ground toe first. *Ui's foot touches the ground toe first.* Good. Excellent. You have a natural gift. Only the arms. They're not quite right. Stiff. Perhaps if you joined your arms in front of your private parts. *Ui joins his arms in front of his private parts.* Not bad. Relaxed but firm. But

head back. Good. Just the right gait for your purposes, I
believe, Mr Ui. What else do you wish to learn?

UI: How to stand. In front of people.

GIVOLA: Have two big bruisers right behind you and you'll
be standing pretty.

UI: That's bunk. When I stand I don't want people looking
at the two bozos behind me. I want them looking at me.
Correct me!

He takes a stance, his arms crossed over his chest.

THE ACTOR: A possible solution. But common. You don't
want to look like a barber, Mr Ui. Fold your arms like this.
*He folds his arms in such a way that the backs of his hands
remain visible. His palms are resting on his arms not far from
the shoulder.* A trifling change, but the difference is in-
calculable. Draw the comparison in the mirror, Mr Ui.
Ui tries out the new position before the mirror.

UI: Not bad.

GIVOLA: What's all this for, boss? Just for those
Fancy-pants in the Trust?

UI: Hell, no! It's for
The little people. Why, for instance, do
You think this Clark makes such a show of grandeur?
Not for his peers. His bank account
Takes care of them, the same as my big bruisers
Lend me prestige in certain situations.
Clark makes a show of grandeur to impress
The little man. I mean to do the same.

GIVOLA: But some will say it doesn't look inborn.
Some people stick at that.

UI: I know they do.
But I'm not trying to convince professors
And smart-alecks. My object is the little
Man's image of his master.

GIVOLA: Don't overdo
The master, boss. Better the democrat
The friendly, reassuring type in shirtsleeves.

UI: I've got old Dogsborough for that.

GIVOLA: His image
Is kind of tarnished, I should say. He's still
An asset on the books, a venerable
Antique. But people aren't as eager as they
Were to exhibit him. They're not so sure
He's genuine. It's like the family Bible
Nobody opens any more since, piously
Turning the yellowed pages with a group
Of friends, they found a dried-out bedbug. But
Maybe he's good enough for Cauliflower.

UI: I decide who's respectable.

GIVOLA: Sure thing, boss.
There's nothing wrong with Dogsborough. We can
Still use him. They haven't even dropped him
At City Hall. The crash would be too loud.

UI: Sitting.

THE ACTOR: Sitting. Sitting is almost the hardest, Mr Ui.
There are men who can walk; there are men who can
stand; but find me a man who can sit. Take a chair with a
back-rest, Mr Ui. But don't lean against it. Hands on thighs,
level with the abdomen, elbows away from body. How
long can you sit like that, Mr Ui?

UI: As long as I please.

THE ACTOR: Then everything's perfect, Mr Ui.

GIVOLA: You know, boss, when old Dogsborough passes
    on
Giri could take his place. He's got the
Popular touch. He plays the funny man
And laughs so loud in season that the plaster
Comes tumbling from the ceiling. Sometimes, though
He does it out of season, as for instance
When you step forward as the modest son of
The Bronx you really were and talk about
Those seven determined youngsters.

UI: Then he laughs?

GIVOLA: The plaster tumbles from the ceiling. Don't
Tell him I said so or he'll think I've got
It in for him. But maybe you could make
Him stop collecting hats.
UI: What kind of hats?
GIVOLA: The hats of people he's rubbed out. And running
Around with them in public. It's disgusting.
UI: Forget it. I would never think of muzzling
The ox that treads my corn. I overlook
The petty foibles of my underlings.
To the actor.
And now to speaking! Speak a speech for me!
THE ACTOR: Shakespeare. Nothing else. Julius Caesar. The
Roman hero. *He draws a little book from his pocket.* What
do you say to Mark Antony's speech? Over Caesar's body.
Against Brutus. The ringleader of Caesar's assassins. A
model of demagogy. Very famous. I played Antony in
Zenith in 1908. Just what you need, Mr Ui. *He takes a
stance and recites Mark Antony's speech line for line.*
Friends, Romans, countrymen, lend me your ears!
*Reading from the little book, Ui speaks the lines after him. Now
and then the actor corrects him, but in the main Ui keeps his
rough staccato delivery.*
THE ACTOR: I come to bury Caesar, not to praise him.
The evil that men do lives after them;
The good is oft interred with their bones;
So let it be with Caesar. The noble Brutus
Hath told you Caesar was ambitious.
If it were so, it was a grievous fault,
And grievously hath Caesar answer'd it.
UI, *continues by himself*:
Here, under leave of Brutus and the rest –
For Brutus is an honourable man;
So are they all, all honourable men –
Come I to speak in Caesar's funeral.
He was my friend, faithful and just to me;

But Brutus says he was ambitious;
And Brutus is an honourable man.
He hath brought many captives home to Rome,
Whose ransoms did the general coffers fill;
Did this in Caesar seem ambitious?
When that the poor have cried, Caesar hath wept;
Ambition should be made of sterner stuff.
Yet Brutus says he was ambitious;
And Brutus is an honourable man.
You all did see that on the Lupercal
I thrice presented him a kingly crown,
Which he did thrice refuse. Was this ambition?
Yet Brutus says he was ambitious;
And sure he is an honourable man.
I speak not to disprove what Brutus spoke,
But here I am to speak what I do know.
You all did love him once, not without cause?
What cause withholds you then, to mourn for him?
During the last lines the curtain slowly falls.
A sign appears.

7

Offices of the Cauliflower Trust. Arturo Ui, Ernesto Roma, Giuseppe Givola, Emanuele Giri and bodyguards. A group of small vegetable dealers is listening to Ui. Old Dogsborough, who is ill, is sitting on the platform beside Ui. In the background Clark.

UI, *bellowing*: Murder! Extortion! Highway robbery!
   Machine-guns sputtering on our city streets!
   People going about their business, law-abiding
   Citizens on their way to City Hall
   To make a statement, murdered in broad daylight!
   And what, I ask you, do our town fathers do?

Nothing! These honourable men are much
Too busy planning their shady little deals
And slandering respectable citizens
To think of law enforcement.
GIVOLA: Hear!
UI: In short
Chaos is rampant. Because if everybody
Can do exactly what he pleases, if
Dog can eat dog without a second thought
I call it chaos. Look. Suppose I'm sitting
Peacefully in my vegetable store
For instance, or driving my cauliflower truck
And someone comes barging not so peacefully
Into my store: 'Hands up!' Or with his gun
Punctures my tyres. Under such conditions
Peace is unthinkable. But once I know
The score, once I recognise that men are not
Innocent lambs, then I've got to find a way
To stop these men from smashing up my shop and
Making me, when it suits them put 'em up
And keep 'em up, when I could use my hands
For better things, for instance, counting pickles.
For such is man. He'll never put aside
His hardware of his own free will, say
For love of virtue, or to earn the praises
Of certain silver tongues at City Hall.
If I don't shoot, the other fellow will.
That's logic. Okay. And maybe now you'll ask:
What's to be done? I'll tell you. But first get
This straight: What you've been doing so far is
Disastrous: Sitting idly at your counters
Hoping that everything will be all right
And meanwhile disunited, bickering
Among yourselves, instead of mustering
A strong defence force that would shield you from
The gangsters' depredations. No, I say

This can't go on. The first thing that's needed
Is unity. The second is sacrifices.
What sacrifices? you may ask. Are we
To part with thirty cents on every dollar
For mere protection? No, nothing doing.
Our money is too precious. If protection
Were free of charge, then yes, we'd be all for it.
Well, my dear vegetable dealers, things
Are not so simple. Only death is free:
Everything else costs money. And that includes
Protection, peace and quiet. Life is like
That, and because it never will be any different
These gentlemen and I (there are more outside)
Have resolved to offer you protection.
Givola and Roma applaud.

                                        But
To show you that we mean to operate
On solid business principles, we've asked
Our partner, Mr Clark here, the wholesaler
Whom you all know, to come here and address you.
*Roma pulls Clark forward. A few of the vegetable dealers
applaud.*
GIVOLA: Mr Clark, I bid you welcome in the name
Of this assembly. Mr Ui is honoured
To see the Cauliflower Trust supporting his
Initiative. I thank you, Mr Clark.
CLARK: We of the Cauliflower Trust observe
Ladies and gentlemen, with consternation
How hard it's getting for you vegetable
Dealers to sell your wares. 'Because,' I hear
You say, 'they're too expensive.' Yes, but why
Are they expensive? It's because our packers
And teamsters, pushed by outside agitators
Want more and more. And that's what Mr Ui
And Mr Ui's friends will put an end to.

FIRST DEALER: But if the little man gets less and less
  How is he going to buy our vegetables?
UI: Your question is a good one. Here's my answer:
  Like it or not, this modern world of ours
  Is inconceivable without the working man
  If only as a customer. I've always
  Insisted that honest work is no disgrace.
  Far from it. It's constructive and conducive
  To profits. As an individual
  The working man has all my sympathy.
  It's only when he bands together, when he
  Presumes to meddle in affairs beyond
  His understanding, such as profits, wages
  Etcetera, that I say: Watch your step
  Brother, a worker is somebody who works.
  But when you strike, when you stop working, then
  You're not a worker any more. Then you're
  A menace to society. And that's
  Where I step in.
  Clark applauds.
                    However, to convince you
  That everything is open and above
  Board, let me call your attention to the presence
  Here of a man well-known, I trust, to
  Everybody here for his sterling honesty
  And incorruptible morality.
  His name is Dogsborough.
  The vegetable dealers applaud a little louder.
                    Mr Dogsborough
  I owe you an incomparable debt
  Of gratitude. Our meeting was the work
  Of Providence. I never will forget –
  Not if I live to be a hundred – how
  You took me to your arms, an unassuming
  Son of the Bronx and chose me for your friend
  Nay more, your son.

He seizes Dogsborough's limply dangling hand and shakes it.
GIVOLA, *in an undertone*: How touching! Father and Son!
GIRI, *steps forward*:
   Well, folks, the boss has spoken for us all.
   I see some questions written on your faces.
   Ask them! Don't worry. We won't eat you. You
   Play square with us and we'll play square with you.
   But get this straight: we haven't got much patience
   With idle talk, especially the kind
   That carps and cavils and finds fault
   With everything. You'll find us open, though
   To any healthy, positive suggestion
   On ways and means of doing what must be done.
   So fire away!
   The vegetable dealers don't breathe a word.
GIVOLA, *unctuously*: And no holds barred. I think
   You know me and my little flower shop.
A BODYGUARD: Hurrah for Givola!
GIVOLA: Okay, then. Do
   You want protection? Or would you rather have
   Murder, extortion and highway robbery?
FIRST DEALER: Things have been pretty quiet lately. I
   Haven't had any trouble in my store.
SECOND DEALER: Nothing's wrong in my place.
THIRD DEALER: Nor in mine.
GIVOLA: That's odd.
SECOND DEALER: We've heard that recently in bars
   Things have been happening just like Mr Ui
   Was telling us, that glasses have been smashed
   And gin poured down the drain in places that
   Refused to cough up for protection. But
   Things have been peaceful in the greengoods business.
   So far at least, thank God.
ROMA: And what about
   Sheet's murder? And Bowl's death? Is that
   What you call peaceful?

SECOND DEALER: But is that connected
With cauliflower, Mr Roma?
ROMA: No. Just a minute.
*Roma goes over to Ui, who after his big speech has been sitting
there exhausted and listless. After a few words he motions to
Giri to join them. Givola also takes part in a hurried whispered
conversation. Then Giri motions to one of the bodyguards and
goes out quickly with him.*
GIVOLA: Friends, I've been asked to tell you that a poor
Unhappy woman wishes to express
Her thanks to Mr Ui in your presence.
*He goes to the rear and leads in a heavily made-up and flashily
dressed woman – Dockdaisy – who is holding a little girl by the
hand. The three stop in front of Ui, who has stood up.*
GIVOLA: Speak, Mrs Bowl.
To the vegetable dealers.
                    It's Mrs Bowl, the young
Widow of Mr Bowl, the late accountant
Of the Cauliflower Trust, who yesterday
While on his way to City Hall to do
His duty, was struck down by hand unknown.
Mrs Bowl!
DOCKDAISY: Mr Ui, in my profound bereavement over my
husband who was foully murdered while on his way to
City Hall in the exercise of his civic duty, I wish to express
my heartfelt thanks for the flowers you sent me and my
little girl, aged six, who has been robbed of her father.
To the vegetable dealers. Gentlemen, I'm only a poor widow
and all I have to say is that without Mr Ui I'd be out in
the street as I shall gladly testify at any time. My little girl,
aged five, and I will never forget it, Mr Ui.
Ui gives Dockdaisy his hand and chucks the child under the chin.
GIVOLA: Bravo!
*Giri wearing Bowl's hat cuts through the crowd, followed by
several gangsters carrying large gasoline cans. They make their
way to the exit.*

UI: Mrs Bowl, my sympathies. This lawlessness
This crime wave's got to stop because . . .

GIVOLA, *as the dealers start leaving*:   Hold it!
The meeting isn't over. The next item
Will be a song in memory of poor Bowl
Sung by our friend James Greenwool, followed by
A collection for the widow. He's a baritone.

*One of the bodyguards steps forward and sings a sentimental song
in which the word 'home' occurs frequently. During the performance the gangsters sit rapt, their heads in their hands, or leaning
back with eyes closed, etc. The meagre applause at the end is
interrupted by the howling of police and fire sirens. A red glow
is seen in a large window in the background.*

ROMA: Fire on the waterfront!

A VOICE: Where?

A BODYGUARD *entering*:   Is there a vegetable
Dealer named Hook in the house?

SECOND DEALER: That's me. What's wrong?

THE BODYGUARD: Your warehouse is on fire.

*Hook, the dealer, rushes out. A few follow him. Others go to the
window.*

ROMA: Hold it!
Nobody leave the room!
To the bodyguard.
                            Is it arson?

THE BODYGUARD: It must be. They've found some gasoline
cans.

THIRD DEALER: Some gasoline cans were taken out of here!

ROMA, *in a rage*: What's that? Is somebody insinuating
We did it?

A BODYGUARD, *pokes his automatic into the man's ribs*:
                  What was being taken out
Of here? Did you see any gasoline cans?

OTHER BODYGUARDS, *to other dealers*:
Did you see any cans? – Did you?

THE DEALERS: Not I . . .
  Me neither.
ROMA: That's better.
GIVOLA, *quickly*:   Ha. The very man
  Who just a while ago was telling us
  That all was quiet on the green goods front
  Now sees his warehouse burning, turned to ashes
  By malefactors. Don't you see? Can you
  Be blind? You've got to get together. And quick!
UI, *bellowing*: Things in this town are looking very sick!
  First murder and now arson! This should show
  You men that no one's safe from the next blow!
  A sign appears.

8

The warehouse fire trial. Press. Judge. Prosecutor. Defence counsel. Young Dogsborough. Giri. Givola. Dockdaisy. Bodyguards. Vegetable dealers and Fish, the accused.

a

Emanuele Giri stands in front of the witness's chair, pointing at Fish, the accused, who is sitting in utter apathy.

GIRI, *shouting*: There sits the criminal who lit the fire!
  When I challenged him he was slinking down the street
  Clutching a gasoline can to his chest.
  Stand up, you bastard, when I'm talking to you.
  Fish is pulled to his feet. He stands swaying.
THE JUDGE: Defendant, pull yourself together. This is a

court of law. You are on trial for arson. That is a very
serious matter, and don't forget it!

FISH, *in a thick voice*: Arlarlarl.

THE JUDGE: Where did you get that gasoline can?

FISH: Arlarl.

*At a sign from the judge an excessively well-dressed, sinister-
looking doctor bends down over Fish and exchanges glances with
Giri.*

THE DOCTOR: Simulating.

DEFENCE COUNSEL: The defence moves that other doctors
be consulted.

THE JUDGE, *smiling*: Denied.

DEFENCE COUNSEL: Mr Giri, how did you happen to be
on the spot when this fire, which reduced twenty-two
buildings to ashes, broke out in Mr Hook's warehouse?

GIRI: I was taking a walk for my digestion.

Some of the bodyguards laugh. Giri joins in the laughter.

DEFENCE COUNSEL: Are you aware, Mr Giri, that Mr Fish,
the defendant, is an unemployed worker, that he had
never been in Chicago before and arrived here on foot the
day before the fire?

GIRI: What? When?

DEFENCE COUNSEL: Is the registration number of your car
XXXXXX?

GIRI: Yes.

DEFENCE COUNSEL: Was this car parked outside Dogsborough's restaurant on 87th Street during the four hours
preceding the fire, and was defendant Fish dragged out of
that restaurant in a state of unconsciousness?

GIRI: How should I know? I spent the whole day on a little
excursion to Cicero, where I met fifty-two persons who
are all ready to testify that they saw me.

The bodyguards laugh.

DEFENCE COUNSEL: Your previous statement left me with
the impression that you were taking a walk for your
digestion in the Chicago waterfront area.

GIRI: Any objection to my eating in Cicero and digesting in Chicago?
Loud and prolonged laughter in which the judge joins. Darkness. An organ plays Chopin's Funeral March *in dance rhythm.*

b

When the lights go on, Hook, the vegetable dealer, is sitting in the witness's chair.

DEFENCE COUNSEL: Did you ever quarrel with the defendant, Mr Hook? Did you ever see him before?
HOOK: Never.
DEFENCE COUNSEL: Have you ever seen Mr Giri?
HOOK: Yes. In the office of the Cauliflower Trust on the day of the fire.
DEFENCE COUNSEL: Before the fire?
HOOK: Just before the fire. He passed through the room with four men carrying gasoline cans.
Commotion on the press bench and among the bodyguards.
THE JUDGE: Would the gentlemen of the press please be quiet.
DEFENCE COUNSEL: What premises does your warehouse adjoin, Mr Hook?
HOOK: The premises of the former Sheet shipyard. There's a passage connecting my warehouse with the shipyard.
DEFENCE COUNSEL: Are you aware, Mr Hook, that Mr Giri lives in the former Sheet shipyard and consequently has access to the premises?
HOOK: Yes. He's the stockroom superintendent.
Increased commotion on the press bench. The bodyguards boo and take a menacing attitude toward Hook, the defence and the press. Young Dogsborough rushes up to the judge and whispers something in his ear.

JUDGE: Order in the court! The defendant is unwell. The court is adjourned.
Darkness. The organ starts again to play Chopin's Funeral March *in dance rhythm.*

c

When the lights go on, Hook is sitting in the witness's chair. He is in a state of collapse, with a cane beside him and bandages over his head and eyes.

THE PROSECUTOR: Is your eysight poor, Hook?
HOOK, *with difficulty*: Yes.
THE PROSECUTOR: Would you say you were capable of recognising anyone clearly and definitely?
HOOK: No.
THE PROSECUTOR: Do you, for instance, recognise this man?
He points at Giri.
HOOK: No.
THE PROSECUTOR: You're not prepared to say that you ever saw him before?
HOOK: No.
THE PROSECUTOR: And now, Hook, a very important question. Think well before you answer. Does your warehouse adjoin the premises of the former Sheet shipyard?
HOOK, *after a pause*: No.
THE PROSECUTOR: That is all.
Darkness. The organ starts playing again.

d

When the lights go on, Dockdaisy is sitting in the witness's chair.

DOCKDAISY, *mechanically*: I recognise the defendant perfectly because of his guilty look and because he is five feet eight inches tall. My sister-in-law has informed me that he was seen outside City Hall on the afternoon my husband was shot while entering City Hall. He was carrying a Webster sub-machine gun and made a suspicious impression.
Darkness. The organ starts playing again.

e

When the lights go on, Giuseppe Givola is sitting in the witness's chair. Greenwool, the bodyguard, is standing near him.

THE PROSECUTOR: It has been alleged that certain men were seen carrying gasoline cans out of the offices of the Cauliflower Trust before the fire. What do you know about this?
GIVOLA: It couldn't be anybody but Mr Greenwool.
THE PROSECUTOR: Is Mr Greenwool in your employ?
GOVOLA: Yes.
THE PROSECUTOR: What is your profession, Mr Givola?
GIVOLA: Florist.
THE PROSECUTOR: Do florists use large quantities of gasoline?
GIVOLA, *seriously*: No, only for plant lice.

THE PROSECUTOR: What was Mr Greenwool doing in the offices of the Cauliflower Trust?

GIVOLA: Singing a song.

THE PROSECUTOR: Then he can't very well have carried any gasoline cans to Hook's warehouse at the same time.

GIVOLA: It's out of the question. It's not in his character to start fires. He's a baritone.

THE PROSECUTOR: If it please the court, I should like witness Greenwool to sing the fine song he was singing in the offices of the Cauliflower Trust while the warehouse was being set on fire.

THE JUDGE: The court does not consider it necessary.

GIVOLA: I protest.

He rises.

The bias in this courtroom is outrageous.
Cleancut young fellows who in broadest daylight
Fire a well-meant shot or two are treated
Like shady characters. It's scandalous.

Laughter. Darkness. The organ starts playing again.

f

When the lights go on, the courtroom shows every indication of utter exhaustion.

THE JUDGE: The press has dropped hints that this court might be subject to pressure from certain quarters. The court wishes to state that it has been subjected to no pressure of any kind and is conducting this trial in perfect freedom. I believe this will suffice.

THE PROSECUTOR: Your Honour! In view of the fact that defendant Fish persists in simulating dementia, the prosecution holds that he cannot be questioned any further. We therefore move . . .

DEFENCE COUNSEL: Your honour. The defendant is coming to!

Commotion.

FISH, *seems to be waking up*: Arlarlwaratarlawatrla.

DEFENCE COUNSEL: Water! Your Honour! I ask leave to question defendant Fish.

Uproar.

THE PROSECUTOR: I object. I see no indication that Fish is in his right mind. It's all a machination on the part of the defence, cheap sensationalism, demagogy!

FISH: Watr.

Supported by the defence counsel, he stands up.

DEFENCE COUNSEL: Fish. Can you answer me?

FISH: Yarl.

DEFENCE COUNSEL: Fish, tell the court: Did you, on the 28th of last month, set fire to a vegetable warehouse on the waterfront? Yes or no?

FISH: N-n-no.

DEFENCE COUNSEL: When did you arrive in Chicago, Fish?

FISH: Water.

DEFENCE COUNSEL: Water!

Commotion. Young Dogsborough has stepped up to the judge and is talking to him emphatically.

GIRI *stands up square-shouldered and bellows*: Frame-up! Lies! Lies!

DEFENCE COUNSEL: Did you ever see this man – *He indicates Giri.* – before?

FISH: Yes. Water.

DEFENCE COUNSEL: Where? Was it in Dogsborough's restaurant on the waterfront?

FISH, *faintly*: Yes.

Uproar. The bodyguards draw their guns and boo. The doctor comes running in with a glass. He pours the contents into Fish's mouth before the defence counsel can take the glass out of his hand.

DEFENCE COUNSEL: I object. I move that this glass be
   examined.
THE JUDGE, *exchanging glances with the prosecutor*: Motion
   denied.
DOCKDAISY *screams at Fish*: Murderer!
DEFENCE COUNSEL: Your Honour!
   Because the mouth of truth cannot be stopped with earth
   They're trying to stop it with a piece of paper
   A sentence to be handed down as though
   Your Honour – that's their hope – should properly
   Be titled Your Disgrace. They cry to justice:
   Hands up! Is this our city, which has aged
   A hundred years in seven days beneath
   The onslaught of a small but bloody brood
   Of monsters, now to see its justice murdered
   Nay, worse than murdered, desecrated by
   Submission to brute force? Your Honour!
   Suspend this trial!
THE PROSECUTOR: I object!
GIRI: You dog!
   You lying, peculating dog! Yourself
   A poisoner! Come on! Let's step outside!
   I'll rip your guts out! Gangster!
DEFENCE COUNSEL: The whole
   Town knows this man.
GIRI, *fuming*:   Shut up!
   When the judge tries to interrupt him:
                              You too!
   Just keep your trap shut if you want to live!
   He runs short of breath and the judge manages to speak.
THE JUDGE: Order in the court. Defence counsel will incur
   charges of contempt of court. Mr Giri's indignation is
   quite understandable. *To the defence counsel*: Continue.
DEFENCE COUNSEL: Fish! Did they give you anything to
   drink at Dogsborough's restaurant? Fish! Fish!

GIEI, *bellowing*: Go on and shout! Looks like his tyre's gone
down.
We'll see who's running things in this here town!
Uproar. Darkness. The organ starts again to play Chopin's
Funeral March *in dance rhythm.*

g

As the lights go on for the last time, the judge stands up and in a
toneless voice delivers the sentence. The defendant is deathly pale.

THE JUDGE: Charles Fish, I find you guilty of arson and
sentence you to fifteen years at hard labour.
A sign appears.

9

a

Cicero. A woman climbs out of a shot-up truck and staggers
forward.

THE WOMAN: Help! Help! Don't run away. Who'll testify?
My husband is in that truck. They got him. Help!
My arm is smashed . . . And so's the truck. I need
A bandage for my arm. They gun us down
Like rabbits. God! Won't anybody help?
You murderers! My husband! I know who's
Behind it. Ui! *Raging*: Fiend! Monster! Shit!
You'd make an honest piece of shit cry out:
Where can I wash myself? You lousy louse!
And people stand for it. And we go under.

Hey you! It's Ui!
A burst of machine-gun fire nearby. She collapses.
Ui did this job!
Where's everybody? Help! who'll stop that mob?

b

Dogsborough's country house. Night toward morning.
Dogsborough is writing his will and confession.

DOGSBOROUGH:
And so I, honest Dogsborough acquiesced
In all the machinations of that bloody gang
After full eighty years of uprightness.
I'm told that those who've known me all along
Are saying I don't know what's going on
That if I knew I wouldn't stand for it.
Alas, I know it all. I know who set
Fire to Hook's warehouse. And I know who dragged
Poor Fish into the restaurant and doped him.
I know that when Sheet died a bloody death
His steamship ticket in his pocket, Roma
Was there. I know that Giri murdered Bowl
That afternoon outside of City Hall
Because he knew too much about myself
Honest old Dogsborough. I know that he
Shot Hook, and saw him with Hook's hat.
I know that Givola committed five
Murders, here itemised. I also know
All about Ui, and I know he knew
All this – the deaths of Sheet and Bowl, Givola's
Murderers and all about the fire. All this
Your honest Dogsborough knew. All this
He tolerated out of sordid lust
For gain, and fear of forfeiting your trust.

Hotel Mammoth. Ui's suite. Ui is sitting slumped in a deep chair,
staring into space. Givola is writing and two bodyguards are looking
over his shoulder, grinning.

GIVOLA: And so I, Dogsborough, bequeath my bar
  To good hard-working Givola. My country
  House to the brave, though somewhat hot-headed Giri.
  And I bequeath my son to honest Roma.
  I furthermore request that you appoint
  Roma police chief, Giri judge, and Givola
  Commissioner of welfare. For my own
  Position I would warmly recommend
  Arturo Ui, who, believe your honest
  Old Dogsborough, is worthy of it. – That's
  Enough, I think, let's hope he kicks in soon.
  This testament will do wonders. Now that the old
  Man's known to be dying and the hope arises
  Of laying him to rest with relative
  Dignity, in clean earth, it's well to tidy up
  His corpse. A pretty epitaph is needed.
  Ravens from olden time have battened on
  The reputation of the fabulous
  White raven that somebody saw sometime
  And somewhere. This old codger's their white raven.
  I guess they couldn't find a whiter one.
  And by the way, boss, Giri for my taste
  Is too much with him. I don't like it.
UI, *starting up*:   Giri?
  What about Giri?

GIVOLA: Only that he's spending
A little too much time with Dogsborough.
UI: I
Don't trust him.
Giri comes in wearing a new hat, Hook's.
GIVOLA: I don't either. Hi, Giri
How's Dogsborough's apoplexy?
GIRI: He refuses
To let the doctor in.
GIVOLA: Our brilliant doctor
Who took such loving care of Fish?
GIRI: No other
Will do. The old man talks too much.
UI: Maybe somebody's talked too much to him . . .
GIRI: What's that? *To Givola:* You skunk, have you been
    stinking up
The air around here again?
GIVOLA, *alarmed:*   Just read the will
Dear Giri.
GIRI, *snatches it from him:*
                What! Police chief? Him? Roma?
You must be crazy.
GIVOLA: He demands it. I'm
Against it too. The bastard can't be trusted
Across the street.
Roma comes in followed by bodyguards.
                Hi, Roma. Take a look at
This will.
ROMA, *grabbing it out of his hands:*
                Okay, let's see it. What do you know!
Giri a judge! But where's the old man's scribble?
GIRI: Under his pillow. He's been trying to
    Smuggle it out. Five times I've caught his son.
ROMA *holds out his hand:*
    Let's have it, Giri.
GIRI: What? I haven't got it.

ROMA: Oh yes, you have!
They glare at each other furiously.
                              I know what's on your mind.
There's something about Sheet. That concerns me.
GIRI: Bowl figures in it too. That concerns *me*.
ROMA: Okay, but you're both jerks, and I'm a man.
I know you, Giri, and you too, Givola.
I'd even say your crippled leg was phony.
Why do I always find you bastards here?
What are you cooking up? What lies have they
Been telling you about me, Arturo? Watch
Your step, you pipsqueaks. If I catch you trying
To cross me up, I'll rub you out like blood spots.
GIRI: Roma, you'd better watch your tongue. I'm not
One of your two-bit gunmen.
ROMA, *to his bodyguards*:   That means you!
That's what they're calling you at headquarters.
They hobnob with the Cauliflower Trust –
Pointing to Giri.
That shirt was made to order by Clark's tailor –
You two-bit gunmen do the dirty work –
And you – *To Ui.* – put up with it.
UI, *as though waking up*:   Put up with what?
GIVOLA: His shooting up Caruther's trucks. Caruther's
A member of the Trust.
UI: Did you shoot up
Caruther's trucks?
ROMA: I gave no orders. Just
Some of the boys. Spontaneous combustion.
They don't see why it's always the small grocers
That have to sweat and bleed. Why not the big wheels?
Damn it, Arturo, I myself don't get it.
GIVOLA: The Trust is good and mad.
GIRI: Clark says they're only
Waiting for it to happen one more time.
He's put in a complaint with Dogsborough.

UI, *morosely*: Ernesto, these things mustn't happen.
GIRI: Crack down, boss!
   These guys are getting too big for their breeches.
GIVOLA: The Trust is good and mad, boss.
ROMA *pulls his gun. To Giri and Givola*:
   Okay. Hands up!
   To their bodyguards:
                                 You too!
   Hands up the lot of you. No monkey business!
   Now back up to the wall.
   *Givola, his men, and Giri raise their hands and with an air of
   resignation back up to the wall.*
UI, *indifferently*:   What is all this?
   Ernesto, don't make them nervous. What are you guys
   Squabbling about? So some palooka's wasted
   Some bullets on a cauliflower truck.
   Such misunderstandings can be straightened out.
   Everything is running smooth as silk.
   The fire was a big success. The stores
   Are paying for protection. Thirty cents
   On every dollar. Almost half the city
   Has knuckled under in five days. Nobody
   Raises a hand against us. And I've got
   Bigger and better projects.
GIVOLA, *quickly*:   Projects? What
   For instance?
GIRI: Fuck your projects. Get this fool
   To let me put my hands down.
ROMA: Safety first, Arturo.
   We'd better leave them up.
GIVOLA: Won't it look sweet
   If Clark comes in and sees us here like this?
UI: Ernesto, put that rod away!
ROMA: No dice!
   Wake up, Arturo. Don't you see their game?
   They're selling you out to the Clarks and Dogsboroughs.

'If Clark comes in and sees us!' What, I ask you
Has happened to the shipyard's funds? We haven't
Seen a red cent. The boys shoot up the stores
Tote gasoline to warehouses and sigh:
We made Arturo what he is today
And he doesn't know us any more. He's playing
The shipyard owner and tycoon. Wake up
Arturo!

GIRI: Right. And speak up. Tell us where
You stand.

UI *jumps up*:   Are you boys trying to pressure me
At gunpoint? Better not, I'm warning you
You won't get anywhere with me like that.
You'll only have yourselves to blame for
The consequences. I'm a quiet man. But
I won't be threatened. Either trust me blindly
Or go your way. I owe you no accounting.
Just do your duty, and do it to the full.
The recompense is up to me, because
Duty comes first and then the recompense.
What I demand of you is trust. You lack
Faith, and where faith is lacking, all is lost.
How do you think I got this far? By faith!
Because of my fanatical, my unflinching
Faith in the cause. With faith and nothing else
I flung a challenge at this city and forced
It to its knees. With faith I made my way
To Dogsborough. With faith I climbed the steps
Of City Hall. With nothing in my naked
Hands but indomitable faith.

ROMA: And
A tommy gun.

UI: No, other men have them
But lack firm faith in their predestination
To leadership. And that is why you too
Need to have faith in me. Have faith! Believe that

I know what's best for you and that I'm
Resolved to put it through. That I will find
The road to victory. If Dogsborough
Passes away, then I decide who gets to
Be what. I say no more, but rest assured:
You'll all be satisfied.

GIVOLA *puts his hand on his heart*:
                              Arturo!

ROMA, *sullenly*:   Scram
   You guys!
   *Giri, Givola and Givola's bodyguard go out slowly with their
   hands up.*

GIRI, *leaving, to* Roma: I like your hat.

GIVOLA, *leaving*:   Dear Roma...

ROMA: Scram!
   Giri, you clown, don't leave your laugh behind.
   And Givola, you crook, be sure to take
   Your clubfoot, though I'm pretty sure you stole it.
   When they are gone, Ui relapses into his brooding.

UI: I want to be alone.

ROMA, *standing still*:   Arturo, if I
   Hadn't the kind of faith you've just described
   I'd sometimes find it hard to look my
   Men in the face. We've got to act. And quickly.
   Giri is cooking up some dirty work.

UI: Don't worry about Giri. I am planning
   Bigger and better things. And now, Ernesto
   To you, my oldest friend and trusted lieutenant
   I will divulge them.

ROMA, *beaming*:   Speak, Arturo. Giri
   And what I had to say of him can wait.
   He sits down with Ui. Roma's men stand waiting in the corner.

UI: We're finished with Chicago. I need more.

ROMA: More?

UI: Vegetables are sold in other cities.

ROMA: But how are you expecting to get in?

UI: Through
   The front door, through the back door, through the
      windows.
   Resisted, sent away, called back again.
   Booed and acclaimed. With threats and supplications
   Appeals and insults, gentle force and steel
   Embrace. In short, the same as here.
ROMA: Except
   Conditions aren't the same in other places.
UI: I have in mind a kind of dress rehearsal
   In a small town. That way we'll see
   Whether conditions are so different. I
   Doubt it.
ROMA: And where have you resolved to stage
   This dress rehearsal?
UI: In Cicero.
ROMA: But there
   They've got this Dullfeet with his Journal
   For Vegetables and Positive Thinking
   Which every Saturday accuses me
   Of murdering Sheet.
UI: That's got to stop.
ROMA: It will. These journalists have enemies.
   Their black and white makes certain people
   See red. Myself, for instance. Yes, Arturo
   I think these accusations can be silenced.
UI: I'm sure they can. The Trust is negotiating
   With Cicero right now. For the time being
   We'll just sell cauliflower peacefully.
ROMA: Who's doing this negotiating?
   UI: Clark.
   But he's been having trouble. On our account.
ROMA: I see. So Clark is in it. I wouldn't trust
   That Clark around the corner.
UI: In Cicero
   They say we're following the Cauliflower

Trust like its shadow. They want cauliflower, but
They don't want us. The shopkeepers don't like us.
A feeling shared by others: Dullfeet's wife
For instance, who for years now has been running
A greengoods wholesale house. She'd like to join
The Trust, and would have joined except for us.
ROMA: You mean this plan of moving in on Cicero
Didn't start with you at all, but with the Trust?
Arturo, now I see it all. I see
Their rotten game.
UI: Whose game?
ROMA: The Trust's.
The goings-on at Dogsborough's! His will!
It's all a machination of the Trust.
They want the Cicero connection. You're in
The way. But how can they get rid of you?
You've got them by the balls, because they needed
You for their dirty business and connived at
Your methods. But now they've found a way:
Old Dogsborough confesses and repairs
In ash and sackcloth to his coffin.
The cauliflower boys with deep emotion
Retrieve this paper from his hands and sobbing
Read it to the assembled press: how he repents
And solemnly adjures them to wipe out
The plague which he – as he confesses – brought
In, and restore the cauliflower trade
To its time-honoured practices.
That's what they plan, Arturo. They're all in it:
Giri, who gets Dogsborough to scribble wills
And who is hand in glove with Clark, who's having
Trouble in Cicero because of us
And wants pure sunshine when he shovels shekels.
Givola, who smells carrion. – This Dogsborough
Honest old Dogsborough with his two-timing will
That splatters you with muck has got to be

Rubbed out, Arturo, or your best-laid plans
For Cicero are down the drain.

UI: You think
It's all a plot? It's true. They've kept me out
Of Cicero. I've noticed that.

ROMA: Arturo
I beg you: let me handle this affair.
I tell you what: my boys and I will beat
It out to Dogsborough's tonight
And take him with us. To the hospital
We'll tell him – and deliver him to the morgue.

UI: But Giri's with him at the villa.

ROMA: He
Can stay there.
They exchange glances.
                    Two birds one stone.

UI: And Givola?

ROMA: On the way back I'll drop in at the florist's
And order handsome wreaths for Dogsborough.
For Giri too, the clown. And I'll pay cash.
He pats his gun.

UI: Ernesto, this contemptible project of
The Dogsboroughs and Clarks and Dullfeets
To squeeze me out of Cicero's affairs
By coldly branding me a criminal
Must be frustrated with an iron hand.
I put my trust in you.

ROMA: And well you may.
But you must meet with us before we start
And give the boys a talk to make them see
The matter in its proper light. I'm not
So good at talking.

UI, *shaking his hand*: It's a deal.

ROMA: I knew it
Arturo. This was how it had to be
Decided. Say, the two of us! Say, you

And me! Like in the good old days.
To his men.
                                    What did
I tell you, boys? He gives us the green light.
UI: I'll be there.
ROMA: At eleven.
UI: Where?
ROMA: At the garage.
I'm a new man. At last we'll see some fight!
He goes out quickly with his men. Pacing the floor, Ui prepares
the speech he is going to make to Roma's men.
UI: Friends, much as I regret to say it, word
Has reached me that behind my back perfidious
Treason is being planned. Men close to me
Men whom I trusted implicitly
Have turned against me. Goaded by ambition
And crazed by lust for gain, these despicable
Fiends have conspired with the cauliflower
Moguls – no, that won't do – with who? I've got it!
With the police, to coldly liquidate you
And even, so I hear, myself. My patience
Is at an end. I therefore order you
Under Ernesto Roma who enjoys
My fullest confidence, tonight . . .
Enter Clark, Giri and Betty Dullfeet.
GIRI, *noticing that Ui looks frightened*: It's only
Us, boss.
CLARK: Ui, let me introduce
Mrs Dullfeet of Cicero. The Trust
Asks you to give her your attention, and hopes
The two of you will come to terms.
UI, *scowling*:   I'm listening.
CLARK: A merger, as you know, is being considered
Between Chicago's Cauliflower Trust
And Cicero's purveyors. In the course
Of the negotiations, Cicero

Objected to your presence on the board.
The Trust was able, after some discussion
To overcome this opposition. Mrs Dullfeet
Is here . . .

MRS DULLFEET: To clear up the misunderstanding.
Moreover, I should like to point out that
My husband, Mr Dullfeet's newspaper
Campaign was not directed against you
Mr Ui.

UI: Against who was it directed?

CLARK: I may as well speak plainly, Ui. Sheet's
'Suicide' made a very bad impression
In Cicero. Whatever else Sheet may
Have been, he was a shipyard owner
A leading citizen, and not some Tom
Dick or Harry whose death arouses no
Comment. And something else. Caruther's
Garage complains of an attack on one of
Its trucks. And one of your men, Ui, is
Involved in both these cases.

MRS DULLFEET: Every child in
Cicero knows Chicago's cauliflower
Is stained with blood.

UI: Have you come here to insult me?

MRS DULLFEET:
No, no. Not you, since Mr Clark has vouched
For you. It's this man Roma.

CLARK, *quickly*:   Cool it, Ui!

GIRI: Cicero . . .

UI: You can't talk to me like this!
What do you take me for? I've heard enough!
Ernesto Roma is my man. I don't
Let anybody tell me who to pal with.
This is an outrage.

GIRI: Boss!

MRS DULLFEET: Ignatius Dullfeet

Will fight the Romas of this world to his
Last breath.
CLARK, *coldly*: And rightly so. In that the Trust
Is solidly behind him. Think it over.
Friendship and business are two separate things.
What do you say?
UI, *likewise coldly*:   You heard me, Mr Clark.
CLARK: Mrs Dullfeet, I regret profoundly
The outcome of this interview.
On his way out, to Ui:
                            Most unwise, Ui.
Left alone, Ui and Giri do not look at each other.
GIRI: This and the business with Caruther's truck
Means war. That's plain.
UI: I'm not afraid of war.
GIRI: Okay, you're not afraid. You'll only have
The Trust, the papers, the whole city, plus
Dogsborough and his crowd against you.
Just between you and me, boss, I'd think twice . . .
UI: I know my duty and need no advice.
A sign appears.

I I

*Garage. Night. The sound of rain. Ernesto Roma and young Inna.
In the background gunmen.*

INNA: It's one o'clock.
ROMA: He must have been delayed.
INNA: Could he be hesitating?
ROMA: He could be.
Arturo's so devoted to his henchmen
He'd rather sacrifice himself than them.
Even with rats like Givola and Giri

He can't make up his mind. And so he dawdles
And wrestles with himself. It might be two
Or even three before he gets a move on.
But never fear, he'll come. Of course he will.
I know him, Inna.
Pause.
                        When I see that Giri
Flat on the carpet, pouring out his guts
I'll feel as if I'd taken a good leak.
Oh well, it won't be long.
INNA: These rainy nights are
Hard on the nerves.
ROMA: That's what I like about them.
Of nights the blackest
Of cars the fastest
And of friends
The most resolute.
INNA: How many years have
You known him?
ROMA: Going on eighteen.
INNA: That's a long time.
A GUNMAN *comes forward*:
The boys want whisky.
ROMA: No. Tonight I need
Them sober.
A little man is brought in by the bodyguards.
THE LITTLE MAN, *out of breath*:
                    Dirty work at the crossroads!
Two armoured cars outside police H.Q.
Jam-packed with cops.
ROMA: Okay, boys, get the
Bullet-proof shutter down. Those cops have got
Nothing to do with us, but foresight's better
Than hindsight.
Slowly an iron shutter falls, blocking the garage door.
                    Is the passage clear?

INNA *nods*: It's a funny thing about tobacco. When a man
  Is smoking, he looks calm. And if you imitate
  A calm-looking man and light a cigarette, you
  Get to be calm yourself.
ROMA, *smiling*:   Hold out your hand.
INNA *does so*: It's trembling. That's no good.
ROMA: Don't worry. It's all
  Right. I don't go for bruisers. They're unfeeling.
  Nothing can hurt them and they won't hurt you.
  Not seriously. Tremble all you like.
  A compass needle is made of steel but trembles
  Before it settles on its course. Your hand
  Is looking for its pole. That's all.
A SHOUT, *from the side*:   Police car
  Coming down Church Street.
ROMA, *intently*:   Is it stopping?
THE VOICE: No.
A GUNMAN *comes in*:
  Two cars with blacked-out lights have turned the corner.
ROMA: They're waiting for Arturo. Givola and
  Giri are laying for him. He'll run straight
  Into their trap. We've got to head him off.
  Let's go!
A GUNMAN: It's suicide.
ROMA: If suicide it is
  Let it be suicide! Hell! Eighteen years
  Of friendship!
INNA, *loud and clear*: Raise the shutter!
  Machine-gun ready?
A GUNMAN: Ready.
INNA: Up she goes.
  The bullet-proof shutter rises slowly. Ui and Givola enter briskly,
  followed by bodyguards.
ROMA: Arturo!
INNA, *under his breath*: Yeah, and Givola.
ROMA: What's up?

Arturo, man, you had us worried. *Laughs loudly*. Hell!
But everything's okay.

UI, *hoarsely*:   Why wouldn't it be okay?

INNA: We thought
Something was wrong. If I were you I'd give him
The glad-hand, boss. He was going to lead
Us all through fire to save you. Weren't you, Roma?
Ui goes up to Roma, holding out his hand. Roma grasps it,
laughing. At this moment, when Roma cannot reach for his gun,
Givola shoots him from the hip.

UI: Into the corner with them!
Roma's men stand bewildered. Inna in the lead, they are driven
into the corner. Givola bends down over Roma, who is lying on the
floor.

GIVOLA: He's still breathing.

UI: Finish him off.
To the men lined up against the wall.
Your vicious plot against me is exposed.
So are your plans to rub out Dogsborough.
I caught you in the nick of time. Resistance
Is useless. I'll teach you to rebel against me!
You bastards!

GIVOLA: Not a single one unarmed!
Speaking of Roma:
He's coming to. He's going to wish he hadn't.

UI: I'll be at Dogsborough's country house tonight.
He goes out quickly.

INNA: You stinking rats! You traitors!

GIVOLA, *excitedly*:   Let 'em have it!
The men standing against the wall are mowed down by machine-
gun fire.

ROMA *comes to:*
Givola! Christ.
Turns over, his face chalky-white.
                    What happened over there?

GIVOLA: Nothing. Some traitors have been executed.

ROMA: You dog! My men! What have you done to them?
Givola does not answer.
And where's Arturo? You've murdered him. I knew it!
Looking for him on the floor.
Where is he?
GIVOLA: He's just left.
ROMA, *as he is being dragged to the wall*: You stinking dogs!
GIVOLA, *coolly*: You say my leg is short, I say your brain is
    small.
Now let your pretty legs convey you to the wall!
A sign appears.

12

*Givola's flower shop. Ignatius Dullfeet, a very small man, and
Betty Dullfeet come in.*

DULLFEET: I don't like this at all.
BETTY: Why not? They've gotten rid
    Of Roma.
DULLFEET: Yes, they've murdered him.
BETTY: That's how
    They do it. Anyway, he's gone. Clark says
    That Ui's years of storm and stress, which even
    The best of men go through, are over. Ui
    Has shown he wants to mend his uncouth ways.
    But if you persevere in your attacks
    You'll only stir his evil instincts up
    Again, and you, Ignatius, will be first
    To bear the brunt. But if you keep your mouth shut
    They'll leave you be.
DULLFEET: I'm not so sure my silence
    Will help.

BETTY: It's sure to. They're not beasts.
Giri comes in from one side, wearing Roma's hat.
GIRI: Hi. Here already? Mr Ui's inside.
He'll be delighted. Sorry I can't stay.
I've got to beat it quick before I'm seen.
I've swiped a hat from Givola.
*He laughs so hard that plaster falls from the ceiling, and goes out,
waving.*
DULLFEET:
Bad when they growl. No better when they laugh.
BETTY: Don't say such things, Ignatius. Not here.
DULLFEET, *bitterly*:   Nor
Anywhere else.
BETTY: What can you do? Already
The rumour's going around in Cicero
That Ui's stepping into Dogsborough's shoes.
And worse, the greengoods men of Cicero
Are flirting with the Cauliflower Trust.
DULLFEET:
And now they've smashed two printing presses on me.
Betty, I've got a dark foreboding.
Givola and Ui come in with outstretched hands.
BETTY: Hi, Ui!
UI: Welcome. Dullfeet!
DULLFEET: Mr Ui
I tell you frankly that I hesitated
To come, because . . .
UI: Why hesitate? A man
Like you is welcome everywhere.
GIVOLA: So is a
Beautiful woman.
DULLFEET: Mr Ui, I've felt
It now and then to be my duty to
Come out against . . .
UI: A mere misunderstanding!
If you and I had known each other from

The start, it never would have happened. It
Has always been my fervent wish that what
Had to be done should be done peacefully.
DULLFEET: Violence . . .
UI: No one hates it more than I do.
If men were wise, there'd be no need of it.
DULLFEET: My aim . . .
UI: Is just the same as mine. We both
Want trade to thrive. The small shopkeeper whose
Life is no bed of roses nowadays
Must be permitted to sell his greens in peace.
And find protection when attacked.
DULLFEET, *firmly*:   And be
Free to determine whether he desires
Protection. I regard that as essential.
UI: And so do I. He's *got* to be free to choose.
Why? Because when he chooses his protector
Freely, and puts his trust in somebody he himself
Has chosen, then the confidence, which is
As necessary in the greengoods trade
As anywhere else, will prevail. That's always been
My stand.
DULLFEET: I'm glad to hear it from your lips.
For, no offence intended, Cicero
Will never tolerate coercion.
UI: Of course not.
No one, unless he has to, tolerates
Coercion.
DULLFEET: Frankly, if this merger with the Trust
Should mean importing the ungodly bloodbath
That plagues Chicago to our peaceful town
I never could approve it.
Pause.
UI: Frankness calls
For frankness, Mr Dullfeet. Certain things
That might not meet the highest moral standards

May have occurred in the past. Such things
Occur in battle. Among friends, however
They cannot happen. Dullfeet, what I want
Of you is only that in the future you should
Trust me and look upon me as a friend
Who never till the seas run dry will forsake
A friend – and, to be more specific, that
Your paper should stop printing these horror stories
That only make bad blood. I don't believe
I'm asking very much.
DULLFEET: It's easy not
To write about what doesn't happen, sir.
UI: Exactly. And if now and then some trifling
Incident should occur, because the earth
Is inhabited by men and not by angels
You will abstain, I hope, from printing lurid
Stories about trigger-happy criminals.
I wouldn't go so far as to maintain that
One of our drivers might not on occasion
Utter an uncouth word. That too is human.
And if some vegetable dealer stands
One of our men to a beer for punctual
Delivery of his carrots, let's not rush
Into print with stories of corruption.
BETTY: Mr
Ui, my husband's human.
GIVOLA: We don't doubt it.
And now that everything has been so amiably
Discussed and settled among friends, perhaps
You'd like to see my flowers . . .
UI, *to Dullfeet*:   After you.
They inspect Givola's flower shop. Ui leads Betty, Givola leads
Dullfeet. In the following they keep disappearing behind the
flower displays. Givola and Dullfeet emerge.
GIVOLA: These, my dear Dullfeet, are Malayan fronds.
DULLFEET: Growing, I see, by little oval ponds.

GIVOLA: Stocked with blue carp that stay stock-still for hours.

DULLFEET: The wicked are insensitive to flowers.
They disappear. Ui and Betty emerge.

BETTY: A strong man needs no force to win his suit.

UI: Arguments carry better when they shoot.

BETTY: Sound reasoning is bound to take effect.

UI: Except when one is trying to collect.

BETTY: Intimidation, underhanded tricks . . .

UI: I prefer to speak of pragmatic politics.
They disappear. Givola and Dullfeet emerge.

DULLFEET: Flowers are free from lust and wickedness.

GIVOLA: Exactly why I love them, I confess.

DULLFEET: They live so quietly. They never hurry.

GIVOLA, *mischievously:*
No problems. No newspapers. No worry.
They disappear. Ui and Betty emerge.

BETTY: They tell me you're as abstinent as a vicar.

UI: I never smoke and have no use for liquor.

BETTY: A saint perhaps when all is said and done.

UI: Of carnal inclinations I have none.
They disappear. Givola and Dullfeet emerge.

DULLFEET: Your life with flowers must deeply satisfy.

GIVOLA: It would, had I not other fish to fry.
They disappear. Ui and Betty emerge.

BETTY: What, Mr Ui, does religion mean to you?

UI: I am a Christian. That will have to do.

BETTY: Yes. But the Ten Commandments, where do they
Come in?

UI: In daily life they don't, I'd say.

BETTY: Forgive me if your patience I abuse
But what exactly are your social views?

UI: My social views are balanced, clear and healthy.
What proves it is: I don't neglect the wealthy.
They disappear. Givola and Dullfeet emerge.

DULLFEET: The flowers have their life, their social calls.

GIVOLA: I'll say they do. Especially funerals!
DULLFEET: Oh, I forgot that flowers were your bread.
GIVOLA: Exactly. My best clients are the dead.
DULLFEET: I hope that's not your only source of trade.
GIVOLA: Some people have the sense to be afraid.
DULLFEET: Violence, Givola, brings no lasting glory.
GIVOLA: It gets results, though.
DULLFEET: That's another story.
GIVOLA: You look so pale.
DULLFEET: The air is damp and close.
GIVOLA: The heavy scent affects you, I suppose.
They disappear. Ui and Betty emerge.
BETTY: I am so glad you two have worked things out.
UI: Once frankness showed what it was all about . . .
BETTY: Foul-weather friends will never disappoint . . .
UI, *putting his arm around her shoulder*:
I like a woman who can get the point.
*Givola and Dullfeet, who is deathly pale, emerge. Dullfeet sees
the hand on his wife's shoulder.*
DULLFEET: Betty, we're leaving.
UI *comes up to him, holding out his hand*:
                              Mr Dullfeet, your
Decision honours you. It will redound to
Cicero's welfare. A meeting between such men
As you and me can only be auspicious.
GIVOLA, *giving Betty flowers*:
Beauty to beauty!
BETTY: Look, how nice, Ignatius!
Oh, I'm so happy. 'Bye, 'bye.
GIVOLA: Now we can
Start going places.
UI, *darkly*:   I don't like that man.
A sign appears.

13

Bells. A coffin is being carried into the Cicero funeral chapel, followed by Betty Dullfeet in widow's weeds, and by Clark, Ui, Giri and Givola bearing enormous wreaths. After handing in their wreaths, Giri and Givola remain outside the chapel. The pastor's voice is heard from inside.

VOICE: And so Ignatius Dullfeet's mortal frame
Is laid to rest. A life of meagrely
Rewarded toil is ended, of toil devoted
To others than the toiler who has left us.
The angel at the gates of heaven will set
His hand upon Ignatius Dullfeet's shoulder
Feel that his cloak has been worn thin and say:
This man has borne the burdens of his neighbours.
And in the city council for some time
To come, when everyone has finished speaking
Silence will fall. For so accustomed are
His fellow citizens to listen to
Ignatius Dullfeet's voice that they will wait
To hear him. 'Tis as though the city's conscience
Had died. This man who met with so untimely
An end could walk the narrow path unseeing.
Justice was in his heart. This man of lowly
Stature but lofty mind created in
His newspaper a rostrum whence his voice
Rang out beyond the confines of our city.
Ignatius Dullfeet, rest in peace! Amen.
GIVOLA: A tactful man: no word of how he died.
GIRI, *wearing Dullfeet's hat*:
A tactful man? A man with seven children.
Clark and Mulberry come out of the chapel.

CLARK: God damn it! Are you mounting guard for fear
The truth might be divulged beside his coffin?
GIVOLA: Why so uncivil, my dear Clark? I'd think
This holy place would curb your temper. And
Besides, the boss is out of sorts. He doesn't
Like the surroundings here.
MULBERRY: You murderers!
Ignatius Dullfeet kept his word – and silence.
GIVOLA: Silence is not enough. The kind of men
We need must be prepared not only to
Keep silent for us but to speak – and loudly.
MULBERRY: What could he say except to call you butchers?
GIVOLA: He had to go. That little Dullfeet was
The pore through which the greengoods dealers oozed
Cold sweat. He stank of it unbearably.
GIRI: And what about your cauliflower? Do
You want it sold in Cicero or don't
You?
MULBERRY: Not by slaughter.
GIRI: Hypocrite, how else?
Who helps us eat the calf we slaughter, eh?
You're funny bastards, clamouring for meat
Then bawling out the cook because he uses
A cleaver. We expect you guys to smack
Your lips and all you do is gripe. And now
Go home!
MULBERRY: A sorry day, Clark, when you brought
These people in.
CLARK: You're telling me?
The two go out, deep in gloom.
GIRI: Boss
Don't let those stinkers keep you from enjoying
The funeral!
GIVOLA: Pst! Betty's coming.
*Leaning on another woman, Betty comes out of the chapel.
Ui steps up to her. Organ music from the chapel.*

UI: Mrs
  Dullfeet, my sympathies.
  She passes him without a word.
GIRI, *bellowing*:   Hey, you!
  She stops still and turns around. Her face is white.
UI: I said, my
  Sympathies, Mrs Dullfeet. Dullfeet – God
  Have mercy on his soul – is dead. But cauliflower –
  Your cauliflower – is still with us. Maybe you
  Can't see it, because your eyes are still
  Blinded with tears. This tragic incident
  Should not, however, blind you to the fact
  That shots are being fired from craven ambush
  On law-abiding vegetable trucks.
  And kerosene dispensed by ruthless hands
  Is spoiling sorely needed vegetables.
  My men and I stand ready to provide
  Protection. What's your answer?
BETTY, *looking heavenward*:   This
  With Dullfeet hardly settled in his grave!
UI: Believe me, I deplore the incident:
  The man by ruthless hand extinguished was
  My friend.
BETTY: The hand that felled him was the hand
  That shook his hand in friendship. Yours!
UI: Am I
  Never to hear the last of these foul rumours
  This calumny which poisons at the root
  My noblest aspirations and endeavours
  To live in harmony with my fellow men?
  Oh, why must they refuse to understand me?
  Why will they not requite my trust? What malice
  To speak of threats when I appeal to reason!
  To spurn the hand that I hold out in friendship!
BETTY: You hold it out to murder.

UI: No!
I plead with them and they revile me.
BETTY: You
Plead like a serpent pleading with a bird.
UI: You've heard her. That's how people talk to me.
It was the same with Dullfeet. He mistook
My warm, my open-hearted offer of friendship
For calculation and my generosity
For weakness. How, alas, did he requite
My friendly words? With stony silence. Silence
Was his reply when what I hoped for
Was joyful appreciation. Oh, how I longed to
Hear him respond to my persistent, my
Well-nigh humiliating pleas for friendship, or
At least for a little understanding, with
Some sign of human warmth. I longed in vain.
My only reward was grim contempt. And even
The promise to keep silent that he gave me
So sullenly and God knows grudgingly
Was broken on the first occasion. Where
I ask you is this silence that he promised
So fervently? New horror stories are being
Broadcast in all directions. But I warn you:
Don't go too far, for even my proverbial
Patience has got its breaking point.
BETTY: Words fail me.
UI: Unprompted by the heart, they always fail.
BETTY: You call it heart that makes you speak so glibly?
UI: I speak the way I feel.
BETTY: Can anybody feel
The way you speak? Perhaps he can. Your murders
Come from the heart. Your blackest crimes are
As deeply felt as other men's good deeds.
As we believe in faith, so you believe in
Betrayal. No good impulse can corrupt you.
Unwavering in your inconstancy!

True to disloyalty, staunch in deception!
Kindled to sacred fire by bestial deeds!
The sight of blood delights you. Violence
Exalts your spirit. Sordid actions move you
To tears, and good ones leave you with deep-seated
Hatred and thirst for vengeance.

UI: Mrs Dullfeet
I always – it's a principle of mine –
Hear my opponent out, even when
His words are gall. I know that in your circle
I'm not exactly loved. My origins –
Never have I denied that I'm a humble
Son of the Bronx – are held against me.
'He doesn't even know,' they say, 'which fork
To eat his fish with. How then can he hope
To be accepted in big business? When
Tariffs are being discussed, or similar
Financial matters, he's perfectly capable
Of reaching for his knife instead of his pen.
Impossible! We can't use such a man!'
My uncouth tone, my manly way of calling
A spade a spade are used as marks against me.
These barriers of prejudice compel me
To bank exclusively on my own achievement.
You're in the cauliflower business. Mrs
Dullfeet, and so am I. There lies the bridge
Between us.

BETTY: And the chasm to be bridged
Is only foul murder.

UI: Bitter experience
Teaches me not to stress the human angle
But speak to you as a man of influence
Speaks to the owner of a greengoods business.
And so I ask you: How's the cauliflower
Business? For life goes on despite our sorrows.

BETTY: Yes, it goes on – and I shall use my life

To warn the people of this pestilence.
I swear to my dead husband that in future
I'll hate my voice if it should say 'Good morning'
Or 'Pass the bread' instead of one thing only:
'Extinguish Ui!'
GIRI, *in a threatening tone*: Don't overdo it, kid!
UI: Because amid the tombs I dare not hope
For milder feelings, I'd better stick to business
Which knows no dead.
BETTY: Oh Dullfeet, Dullfeet! Now
I truly know that you are dead.
UI: Exactly.
Bear well in mind that Dullfeet's dead. With him
Has died the only voice in Cicero
That would have spoken out in opposition
To crime and terror. You cannot deplore
His loss too deeply. Now you stand defenceless
In a cold world where, sad to say, the weak
Are always trampled. You've got only one
Protector left. That's me, Arturo Ui.
BETTY: And this to me, the widow of the man
You murdered! Monster! Oh, I knew you'd be here
Because you've always gone back to the scene of
Your crimes to throw the blame on others. 'No
It wasn't me, it was somebody else.'
'I know of nothing.' 'I've been injured'
Cries injury. And murder cries: 'A murder!
Murder must be avenged!'
UI: My plan stands fast.
Protection must be given to Cicero.
BETTY, *feebly*: You won't succeed.
UI: I will. That much I know.
BETTY: From this protector God protect us!
UI: Give
Me your answer.

He holds out his hand.
                    Is it friendship?
BETTY: Never while I live!
Cringing with horror, she runs out.
A sign appears.

14

*Ui's bedroom at the Hotel Mammoth. Ui tossing in his bed,
plagued by a nightmare. His bodyguards are sitting in chairs, their
revolvers on their laps.*

UI, *in his sleep*: Out, bloody shades! Have pity! Get you gone!
    *The wall behind him becomes transparent. The ghost of Ernesto
    Roma appears, a bullet-hole in his forehead.*
ROMA: It will avail you nothing. All this murder
    This butchery, these threats and slaverings
    Are all in vain, Arturo, for the root of
    Your crimes is rotten. They will never flower.
    Treason is made manure. Murder, lie
    Deceive the Clarks and slay the Dullfeets, but
    Stop at your own. Conspire against the world
    But spare your fellow conspirators.
    Trample the city with a hundred feet
    But trample not the feet, you treacherous dog!
    Cozen them all, but do not hope to cozen
    The man whose face you look at in the mirror!
    In striking me, you struck yourself, Arturo!
    I cast my lot with you when you were hardly
    More than a shadow on a bar-room floor.
    And now I languish in this drafty
    Eternity, while you sit down to table
    With sleek and proud directors. Treachery
    Made you, and treachery will unmake you.

Just as you betrayed Ernesto Roma, your
Friend and lieutenant, so you will betray
Everyone else, and all, Arturo, will
Betray you in the end. The green earth covers
Ernesto Roma, but not your faithless spirit
Which hovers over tombstones in the wind
Where all can see it, even the grave-diggers.
The day will come when all whom you struck down
And all you will strike down will rise, Arturo
And, bleeding but made strong by hate, take arms
Against you. You will look around for help
As I once looked. Then promise, threaten, plead.
No one will help. Who helped me in my need?
UI, *jumping up with a start*:
Shoot! Kill him! Traitor! Get back to the dead!
The bodyguards shoot at the spot on the wall indicated by Ui.
ROMA, *fading away*:
What's left of me is not afraid of lead.

15

*Financial District. Meeting of the Chicago vegetable dealers.
They are deathly pale.*

FIRST VEGETABLE DEALER:
Murder! Extortion! Highway robbery!
SECOND VEGETABLE DEALER:
And worse: Submissiveness and cowardice!
THIRD VEGETABLE DEALER:
What do you mean, submissiveness? In January
When the first two came barging into
My store and threatened me at gunpoint, I
Gave them, a steely look from top to toe
And answered firmly: I incline to force.

I made it plain that I could not approve
Their conduct or have anything to do
With them. My countenance was ice.
It said: So be it, take your cut. But only
Because you've got those guns.

FOURTH VEGETABLE DEALER: Exactly!
I wash my hands in innocence! That's what
I told my missus.

FIRST VEGETABLE DEALER, *vehemently*:
What do you mean, cowardice?
We used our heads. If we kept quiet, gritted
Our teeth and paid, we thought those bloody fiends
Would put their guns away. But did they? No! It's
Murder! Extortion! Highway robbery!

SECOND VEGETABLE DEALER:
Nobody else would swallow it. No backbone!

FIFTH VEGETABLE DEALER:
No tommy gun, you mean. I'm not a gangster.
My trade is selling greens.

THIRD VEGETABLE DEALER: My only hope
Is that the bastard some day runs across
Some guys who show their teeth. Just let him try his
Little game somewhere else!

FOURTH VEGETABLE DEALER: In Cicero
For instance.

The Cicero vegetable dealers come in. They are deathly pale.

THE CICERONIANS: Hi, Chicago!

THE CHICAGOANS: Hi, Cicero!
What brings *you* here?

THE CICERONIANS: We were told to come.

THE CHICAGOANS: By who?

THE CICERONIANS: By him.

FIRST CHICAGOAN: Who says so? How can he command
You? Throw his weight around in Cicero?

FIRST CICERONIAN: With
His gun.

SECOND CICERONIAN: Brute force. We're helpless.
FIRST CHICAGOAN: Stinking
   cowards!
   Can't you be men? Is there no law in Cicero?
FIRST CICERONIAN: No.
SECOND CICERONIAN: No longer.
THIRD CHICAGOAN: Listen, friends. You've got
   To fight. This plague will sweep the country
   If you don't stop it.
FIRST CHICAGOAN: First one city, then anotner.
   Fight to the death! You owe it to your country.
SECOND CICERONIAN:
   Why us? We wash our hands in innocence.
FOURTH CHICAGOAN:
   We only hope with God's help that the bastard
   Some day comes across some guys that show
   Their teeth.
   Fanfares. Enter Arturo Ui and Betty Dullfeet – in mourning –
   followed by Clark, Giri, Givola and bodyguards. Flanked by
   the others, Ui passes through. The bodyguards line up in the
   background.
GIRI: Hi, friends! Is everybody here
   From Cicero?
FIRST CICERONIAN: All present.
GIRI: And Chicago?
FIRST CHICAGOAN: All present.
GIRI, *to Ui*:   Everybody's here.
GIVOLA: Greetings, my friends. The Cauliflower Trust
   Wishes you all a hearty welcome. Our
   First speaker will be Mr Clark. *To Clark*: Mr Clark.
CLARK: Gentlemen, I bring news. Negotiations
   Begun some weeks ago and patiently
   Though sometimes stormily pursued – I'm telling
   Tales out of school – have yielded fruit. The wholesale
   House of I. Dullfeet, Cicero, has joined
   The Cauliflower Trust. In consequence

The Cauliflower Trust will now supply
Your greens. The gain for you is obvious:
Secure delivery. The new prices, slightly
Increased, have already been set. It is
With pleasure, Mrs Dullfeet, that the Trust
Welcomes you as its newest member.
Clark and Betty Dullfeet shake hands.
GIVOLA: And now: Arturo Ui.
Ui steps up to the microphone.
UI: Friends, countrymen!
Chicagoans and Ciceronians! When
A year ago old Dogsborough, God rest
His honest soul, with tearful eyes
Appealed to me to protect Chicago's green-
Goods trade, though moved, I doubted whether
My powers would be able to justify
His smiling confidence. Now Dogsborough
Is dead. He left a will which you're all free
To read. In simple words therein he calls me
His son. And thanks me fervently for all
I've done since I responded to his appeal.
Today the trade in vegetables –
Be they kohlrabi, onions, carrots or what
Have you – is amply protected in Chicago.
Thanks, I make bold to say, to resolute
Action on my part. When another civic
Leader, Ignatius Dullfeet, to my surprise
Approached me with the same request, this time
Concerning Cicero, I consented
To take that city under my protection.
But one condition I stipulated, namely:
The dealers had to want me. I would come
Only pursuant to their free decision
Freely arrived at. Cicero, I told
My men, in no uncertain terms, must not be
Subjected to coercion or constraint.

The city has to elect me in full freedom.
I want no grudging 'Why not?', no teeth-gnashing
'We might as well'. Half-hearted acquiescence
Is poison in my books. What I demand
Is one unanimous and joyful 'Yes'
Succinct and, men of Cicero, expressive.
And since I want this and everything else I want
To be complete, I turn again to you
Men of Chicago, who, because you know
Me better, hold me, I have reason to believe
In true esteem, and ask you: Who is for me?
And just in passing let me add: If anyone's
Not for me he's against me and has only
Himself to blame for anything that happens.
Now you may vote.

GIVOLA: But first a word from Mrs
Dullfeet, the widow, known to all of you, of
A man beloved by all.

BETTY: Dear friends
Your faithful friend and my beloved husband
Ignatius Dullfeet is no longer with us to . . .

GIVOLA: God rest his soul!

BETTY: . . . sustain and help you. I
Advise you all to put your trust in Mr
Ui, as I do now that in these grievous days
I've come to know him better.

GIVOLA: Time to vote!

GIRI: All those in favour of Arturo Ui
Raise your right hands!
Some raise their hands.

A CICERONIAN: Is it permissible to leave?

GIVOLA: Each man
Is free to do exactly as he pleases.
*Hesitantly the Ciceronian goes out. Two bodyguards follow him.
A shot is heard.*

GIRI: All right, friends, Let's have your free decision!
All raise both hands.
GIVOLA: They've finished voting, boss. With deep
    emotion
Teeth chattering for joy, the greengoods dealers
Of Cicero and Chicago thank you
For your benevolent protection.
UI: ·   With
Pride I accept your thanks. Some fifteen years
Ago, when I was only a humble, unemployed
Son of the Bronx; when following the call
Of destiny I sallied forth with only
Seven staunch men to brave the Windy City
I was inspired by an iron will
To create peace in the vegetable trade.
We were a handful then, who humbly but
Fanatically strove for this ideal
Of peace! Today we are a multitude.
Peace in Chicago's vegetable trade
Has ceased to be a dream. Today it is
Unvarnished reality. And to secure
This peace I have put in an order
For more machine-guns, rubber truncheons
Etcetera. For Chicago and Cicero
Are not alone in clamouring for protection.
There are other cities: Washington and Milwaukee!
Detroit! Toledo! Pittsburgh! Cincinnati!
And other towns where vegetables are traded!
Philadelphia! Columbus! Charleston! And New York!
They all demand protection! And no 'Phooey!'
No 'That's not nice!' will stop Arturo Ui!
Amid drums and fanfares the curtain falls.
A sign appears.

Epilogue

Therefore learn how to see and not to gape.
To act instead of talking all day long.
The world was almost won by such an ape!
The nations put him where his kind belong.
But don't rejoice too soon at your escape –
The womb he crawled from still is going strong.

Chronological Table

1. 1929–1932. Germany is hard hit by the world crisis. At the height of the crisis a number of Prussian Junkers try to obtain government loans, for a long time without success. The big industrialists in the Ruhr dream of expansion.

2. By way of winning President Hindenburg's sympathy for their cause, the Junkers make him a present of a landed estate.

3. In the autumn of 1932, Adolf Hitler's party and private army are threatened with bankruptcy and disintegration. To save the situation Hitler tries desperately to have himself appointed Chancellor, but for a long time Hindenburg refuses to see him.

4. In January 1933 Hindenburg appoints Hitler Chancellor in return for a promise to prevent the exposure of the Osthilfe (East Aid) scandal, in which Hindenburg himself is implicated.

5. After coming to power legally, Hitler surprises his high patrons by extremely violent measures, but keeps his promises.

6. The gang leader quickly transforms himself into a statesman. He is believed to have taken lessons in declamation and bearing from one, Basil, a provincial actor.

7. February 1933, the Reichstag fire. Hitler accuses his enemies of instigating the fire and gives the signal for the Night of the Long Knives.

8. The Supreme Court in Leipzig condemns an unemployed worker to death for causing the fire. The real incendiaries get off scot-free.

9. and 10. The impending death of the aged Hindenburg provokes bitter struggles in the Nazi camp. The Junkers

and industrialists demand Röhm's removal. The occupation of Austria is planned.

11. On the night of 30 June 1934 Hitler overpowers his friend Röhm at an inn where Röhm has been waiting for him. Up to the last moment Röhm thinks that Hitler is coming to arrange for a joint strike against Hindenburg and Göring.

12. Under compulsion the Austrian Chancellor Engelbert Dollfuss agrees to stop the attacks on Hitler that have been appearing in the Austrian press.

13. Dollfuss is murdered at Hitler's instigation, but Hitler goes on negotiating with Austrian rightist circles.

15. On 11 March 1938 Hitler marches into Austria. An election under the Nazi terror results in a 98% vote for Hitler.

Notes and Variants

Texts by Brecht

INSTRUCTIONS FOR PERFORMANCE

In order that the events may retain the significance unhappily due them, the play must be performed in the grand style, and preferably with obvious harkbacks to the Elizabethan theatre, i.e., with curtains and different levels. For instance, the action could take place in front of curtains of whitewashed sacking spattered the colour of ox blood. At some points panorama-like backdrops could be used, and organ, trumpet, and drum effects are likewise permissible. Use should be made of the masks, vocal characteristics, and gestures of the originals; pure parody however must be avoided, and the comic element must not preclude horror. What is needed is a three-dimensional presentation which goes at top speed and is composed of clearly defined groupings like those favoured by historical tableaux at fairs.

['Hinweis für die Aufführung,' from GW *Stücke*, pp. 1837–38.]

ALTERNATIVE PROLOGUES

Friends, tonight we're going to show –
Pipe down, you boys in the back row!
And madam, your hat is in the way –
Our great historical gangster play
Containing, for the first time, as you'll see
THE TRUTH ABOUT THE SCANDALOUS DOCK SUBSIDY.
Further, we give you for your betterment
DOGSBOROUGH'S CONFESSION AND TESTAMENT.
ARTURO UI'S RISE WHILE THE STOCK MARKET FELL
THE NOTORIOUS WAREHOUSE FIRE TRIAL, WHAT A SELL!
THE DULLFEET MURDER! JUSTICE IN A COMA!
GANG WARFARE: THE KILLING OF ERNESTO ROMA!
All culminating in our stunning last tableau:
GANGSTERS TAKE OVER THE TOWN OF CICERO!
Brilliant performers will portray
The most eminent gangsters of our day
All the hanged and the shot

Disparaged but not
Wholly forgotten gangsters
Taken as models by our youngsters.
Ladies and gentlemen, the management knows
There are ticklish subjects which some of those
Who pay admission hardly love
To be reminded of.
Accordingly we've decided to put on
A story in these parts little known
That took place in another hemisphere –
The kind of thing that's never happened here.
This way you're safe; no chance you'll see
The senior members of your family
In flesh and blood before your eyes
Doing things that aren't too nice.
So just relax, young lady. Don't run away.
You're sure to like our gangster play.

['Prolog (2)' from GW *Stücke*, pp. 1838–39. Written
subsequently to the first version of the play, which includes the prologue given in our text.]

Ladies and gentlemen, the management's aware
This is a controversial affair.
Though some can still take history as they find it
Most of you don't care to be reminded.
Now, ladies and gentlemen, surely what this shows is
Excrescences need proper diagnosis
Conveyed not in some polysyllabic word
But in plain speech that calls a turd a turd.
Never mind if you're used to something more ethereal –
The language of this play suits its material.
Down from your gallows, then! Up from your graves!
You murderous pack of filthy swindling knaves!
Let's see you in the flesh again tonight
And hope that in our present sorry plight
Seeing the men from whom that plight first came
Moves us not just to anger but to shame.

[BBA 174/131. Inserted at the end of the first version of

the play, but evidently written for a German audience after the end of the Second World War.]

NOTES

1. Preface

The Resistible Rise of Arturo Ui, written in Finland in 1941, represents an attempt to make Hitler's rise intelligible to the capitalist world by transposing that rise into a sphere thoroughly familiar to it. The blank verse is an aid in appraising the characters' heroism.

2. Remarks

Nowadays ridiculing the great political criminals, alive or dead, is generally said to be neither appropriate nor constructive. Even the common people are said to be sensitive on this point, not just because they too were implicated in the crimes in question but because it is not possible for those who survived among the ruins to laugh about such things. Nor is it much good hammering at open doors (as there are too many of these among the ruins anyway): the lesson has been learned, so why go on dinning it into the poor creatures? If on the other hand the lesson has not been learned it is risky to encourage a people to laugh at a potentate after once failing to take him seriously enough; and so on and so forth.

It is relatively easy to dismiss the suggestion that art needs to treat brutality with kid gloves; that it should devote itself to watering the puny seedlings of awareness; that it ought to be explaining the garden hose to former wielders of the rubber truncheon, and so on. Likewise it is possible to object to the term 'people,' as used to signify something 'higher' than population, and to show how the term conjures up the notorious concept of *Volksgemeinschaft*, or a 'sense of being one people,' that links executioner and victim, employer and employed. But this does not mean that the suggestion that satire should not meddle in serious matters is an acceptable one. Serious things are its specific concern.

The great political criminals must be completely stripped bare and exposed to ridicule. Because they are not great political criminals at all, but the perpetrators of great political crimes, which is something very different.

There is no need to be afraid of truisms so long as they are true. If the collapse of Hitler's enterprises is no evidence that he was a halfwit, neither is their scale any guarantee that he was a great man. In the main the classes that control the modern state use utterly average people for their enterprises. Not even in the highly important field of economic exploitation is any particular talent called for. A multimillion-Mark trust like I. G. Farben makes use of exceptional intelligence only when it can exploit it; the exploiters proper, a handful of people most of whom acquired their power by birth, have a certain cunning and brutality as a group but see no commercial drawbacks in lack of education, nor even in the presence among them of the odd amiable individual. They get their political affairs dealt with by people often markedly stupider than themselves. Thus Hitler was no doubt a lot more stupid than Brüning, and Brüning than Stresemann, while on the military plane Keitel and Hindenburg were much of a muchness. A military specialist like Ludendorff, who lost battles by his political immaturity, is no more to be thought of as an intellectual giant than is a lightning calculator from the music-hall. It is the scope of their enterprises that gives such people their aura of greatness. But this aura does not necessarily make them all that effective, since it only means that there is a vast mass of intelligent people available, with the result that wars and crises become displays of the intelligence of the entire population.

On top of that it is a fact that crime itself frequently provokes admiration. I never heard the petty bourgeoisie of my home town speak with anything but respectful enthusiasm of a man called Kneisel who was a mass murderer, with the result that I have remembered his name to this day. It was not even thought necessary on his behalf to invent the usual acts of kindness towards poor old grannies: his murders were enough.

In the main the petty bourgeois conception of history (and the proletariat's too, so long as it has no other), is a romantic one. What fired these Germans' poverty-stricken imagination in the case of Napoleon I was of course not his Code Napoléon but his millions of victims. Bloodstains embellish these conquerors' faces like beauty spots. When a certain Dr. Pechel, writing in the aptly named *Deutsche Rundschau* in 1946, said of Genghis Khan that 'the price of the Pax Mongolica was the death of several dozen million men and the destruction of twenty kingdoms,' it made a great man of this 'bloodstained conqueror, the demolisher of all values, though this must not cause us to forget the ruler who showed that his real nature was not destructive' – on the mere grounds that he was never small in his dealings with people. It is this reverence for killers that has to be done away with. Plain everyday logic must never let itself be overawed once it goes strolling among the centuries; whatever applies to small situations must be made to apply to big ones too. The petty rogue whom the rulers permit to become a rogue on the grand scale can occupy a special position in roguery, but not in our attitude to history. Anyway there is truth in the principle that comedy is less likely than tragedy to omit to take human suffering seriously enough.

3. Jottings

Kusche: '... but at the very point where the projections unmistakably relate *Ui* to a specific phase of German history ... the question arises: "Where is the People?"'

'Brecht has written, apropos of Eisler's *Faustus*, that "our starting point has to be the truth of the phrase 'no conception can be valid that assumes German history to be unalloyed *misère* and fails to present the People as a creative force'."'

'What is lacking is something or other that would stand for this "creative force of the People" ... Was it all a mere internal affray between gangsters and merchants? Was Dimitroff (as it is simpler to give that force an individual name) a merchant?'

Ui is a *parable* play, written with the aim of destroying the dangerous respect commonly felt for great killers. The circle described has been deliberately restricted; it is confined to the plane of state, industrialists, Junkers and petty bourgeois. This is enough to achieve the desired objective. The play does not pretend to give a complete account of the historical situation in the 1930s. The proletariat is not present, nor could it be taken into account more than it is, since anything *extra* in this complex would be *too much*; it would distract from the tricky problem posed. (How could more attention be paid to the proletariat without considering unemployment, and how could that be done

without dealing with the [Nazi] employment programme, likewise with the political parties and their abdication? One thing
would entail another, and the result would be a gigantic work
which would fail to do what was intended.)

The projected texts—which K. takes as a reason for expecting
the play to give a general account of what happened – seem to me,
if anything, to stress the element of selectivity, of a peep-show.

The industrialists all seem to have been hit by the crisis to the
same extent, whereas the stronger ought to knock out the weaker.
(But that may be another point which would involve us in too
much detail and which a *parable* can legitimately skip.) The
defence counsel in scene 9 [our scene 8], the warehouse fire trial,
possibly needs another look. At present his protests seem
designed merely to defend a kind of 'honour of the profession'.
The audience will of course want to see him as Dimitroff,
whether it was meant to or not.

As for the appearance of Röhm's ghost, I think Kusche is
right. ('As the text now stands it makes a drunken Nazi slob
look like a martyr.') [. . .]

The play was written in 1941 and conceived as a 1941 production. [. . .]

[From GW *Schriften zum Theater*, pp. 1176–80. Written for a
proposed volume of the *Versuche* whose preparation was interrupted by Brecht's death in 1956. Since the play was first
published in *Sinn und Form* only after that date, the characteristic
East German criticisms voiced by Lothar Kusche (and originally made at a meeting between Brecht and younger writers
in late 1953) must have been based on a reading of the script.]

Later Texts

NOTES BY MANFRED WEKWERTH

1. Lessons of a pilot production at another theatre

Scene 1 [1a]

The members of the trust display the same gangsters' attitudes and costumes as we know from American films; two-tone suits, a variety of hats, scarves, and so on. This misses the point, essential to the story, that here we have old-established business-men who have been in the trade 'since Noah's ark.' These trust members are too much like parvenus, profiteers, so that the element of solid respectability – the bourgeois element – is lost. As a result their subsequent alliance with Ui, far from being worthy of remark, seems natural. Gangsters seeking out their own kind: *not* the bourgeois state turning to something it had expressly branded as its own mortal enemy – organized crime.

For the same reasons the crisis too is ill-founded, since people who make such an impression are used to running into money troubles, because their business (profiteering) involves risks.

Scene 2 [1b]

Ui, Roma, and Ragg emerge on to the apron from below stage and hurry past Clark one by one. In this way they formally announce themselves as gangsters emerging from a sewer man-hole and not, as the story demands, as gangsters offering their services to the trust in a particularly offhand and gentleman-like manner.

Scene 3 [2]. Dogsborough's Restaurant

Unless Dogsborough appears above all as an immovable, un-changeable, impregnable, rocklike fortress (i.e., solidly or im-movably set in an attitude which, to judge from the text, Brecht took from Hindenburg), the great turning point where he crumbles will not be properly brought out, Instead of a 'great personality' succumbing to an economic force we get an average personality doing what is only to be expected. The actor gave us a lively, forceful, decisive, far too young Dogsborough, with an agile mind and agile gestures. When he looked out of the window and succumbed to the house by the lake, he turned round at least two times in order to express his reservations, and in so doing destroyed the great instant of succumbing.

Similarly with Dogsborough's treatment by the trust people. They should not address him as if he were one of their own sort – i.e., in business jargon – but ought to deploy considerable human resources in order to get him to listen to them at all. They should all the time be confirming his reputation as honest old Dogsborough.

As to the identification of the characters with the Nazi leaders: Dogsborough bore no kind of resemblance to Hindenburg, neither of attitude, gesture, tone of voice, nor mask. The necessary degree of likeness to Hindenburg could only be achieved once one had taken in the inscriptions, and after the play had ended. The highly amusing way in which the course of the action instantly and directly alienates the gangsters into top Nazis was missed, or at any rate seemed vague and inexact.

The play was written against Hitler and the big shots of those times. No general conclusions can be drawn until this story, transposed into terms of the gang world, can be concretely recognized so as to allow people in subsequent times to generalize from concrete knowledge and detect fascist trends. To start off by generalizing – i.e., by making the characters identifiable not merely with Hitler and Hindenburg – makes the events less concrete and prevents any true historical generalization. This is particularly true of our own time, where the historical events are barely remembered and the top Nazis virtually unknown except from photographs. Brecht himself rejects such a discreet approach inasmuch as he uses allusive names (Dogsborough, Giri, Roma, etc.), and calls for prescribed similarities of voice, gesture, and masks. Without this, the work degenerates into a *roman à clef*.

Scene 4 [3]. Bookmaker's office
In the bookmaker's office the group of leaders – Ui, Ragg, and

Roma – associated with the other gangsters, with the result that their discussions degenerated into everyday conversation instead of being a crucial conversation between leading personalities; for the crisis would hardly be discussed before all and sundry. This was accentuated by the unrelievedly pliable, deflated, rubbery, unassertive attitude of Arturo Ui, who was in no way shown as a boss, but more as a passive plaything among strong men. Presented in such a wretched niggling light, his plans did not emerge as dangerous; what was shown was not so much the large-scale planning of lunacy as the actual lunacy itself. This meant that the Nazis' logical approach – which admittedly developed on a basis of lunacy and lack of logic – was never established, so that every subsequent action seemed more or less accidental and not thought up with a vast expenditure of effort. Hence Nazism emerged as haphazard and individualistic instead of being a system: a system based on lunacy and lack of system.

Puny swindles ought to be mightily pondered underhand actions conceived on a vast scale; instances of thoughtlessness realized by enormous thought.

Ui as a character

Ui was presented as a passive plaything in the hands of strong men (Goebbels, Göring, Papen). He has pathological features which ran unchanged right through the play. All through he gave evidence of exhaustion and lack of enterprise, needing to be prompted and jogged by Givola even during his big speeches. In this way the character was emasculated and the main weight of responsibility shifted to the strong men, but without any explanation why they in particular should be strong.

One of the dangerous things about Hitler was his immensely stubborn logic, a logic based on absence of logic, lack of understanding, and half-baked ideas. (Even the concentration camps were no accidental creation, having been planned as early as 1923.) Precisely Hitler's languidness, his indecision, emptiness, feebleness, and freedom from ideas were the source of his usefulness and strength.

The impression given in this production was that Hitler's feebleness and malleability were a liability to the movement, and that given greater energy and intelligence fascism would have proved much easier to put up with, since its shortcomings were here attributed to human weakness. [. . .]

[. . .]

The investigation [Scene 5]

The legal process failed to come across. It was impossible to tell who has convened the inquiry, who is being accused, what part is being played by Dogsborough, how far an appearance of justice still matters, what official standing Ui has there. This scene accordingly came across as a muddle, not as a bourgeois legal ritual that gangsters can use unchanged. Rituals and arrangements should therefore be portrayed with especial precision and care. Only the dignity of the traditional procedures can show the indignity of what is taking place.

The Warehouse Fire Trial [Scene 8]

This scene was not helped by the symbolic grouping which had the populace represented by Nazis who stood a few inches behind the centrally placed judges (pointing a pistol at their heads!).

The fact that the Nazis needed the seal of approval of the bourgeois court, along with its dignity and its traditions, was thereby made incomprehensible. Instead it became an unceremonious gang tribunal, and accordingly without any meaning as a court.

If all that is to appear is how the court's bourgeois traditions are flouted, then it becomes impossible to show how the bourgeois court, by the mere fact of its existence, flouts justice; how crime is an integral part of its traditional procedures; and how it is unnecessary for this tradition to be broken to make it criminal.

[From Manfred Wekwerth: *Schriften*, Arbeit mit Brecht, East Berlin, Henschel-Verlag, 1973, pp. 144-7. The production in question was that of the world première at Stuttgart under Peter Palitzsch's direction in November 1958, a pilot for the subsequent Berliner Ensemble production directed by Palitzsch and Wekwerth together.]

2. Two notes on the Berliner Ensemble production

(a) The historical references

After the third rehearsal we gave up trying to base the principal parts on their correspondences with the Nazi originals. The mistake became particularly evident in the case of Schall, who gave an extremely well-observed imitation of Hitler's vocal characteristics and gestures, such as we had seen a day or two before on film. The faithfulness of this imitation wholly swamped the story of the gangster play. What resulted was a highly amusing detailed parody, but of details from a play about Nazis. The more profoundly amusing point – the parallel between Nazis and gangsters – was lost, since it can only be made if the gangster story is sufficiently complete and independent to match the Nazi story. It is the distancing of the one story from the other that allows them to be connected up on a historical-philosophical, not a merely mechanical plane. We asked the actors to be guided by a strong sense of fun, free from all historical ideas, in exploiting their extensive knowledge of American gangster movies, then carefully on top of that to put recognizable quotations from the vocal characteristics and gestures of the Nazi originals, rather as one puts on a mask.

(b) About the music

The basic character of the music was dictated by setting the 'great historical gangster play' of the prologue within the colourful shooting-gallery framework of a fairground. At the same time it was the music's job to stress the atmosphere of horror. It had to be garish and nasty.

This suggested the use of pieces of music abused by the Nazis, e.g., the theme from Liszt's *Les Preludes* which they degraded into a signature tune for special announcements on the radio. The idea of playing Chopin's 'Funeral March' at set intervals throughout the long-drawn-out warehouse fire trial was suggested by Brecht. Tempi and rhythms of these themes were of course radically altered to accord with the basic character established for the production.

The orchestra consisted of just a few instruments: trumpet, trombone, tuba, horn, piccolo, clarinet, electric guitar, saxophone, piano, harmonium and percussion.

The sharpness and the fairground effect were furthered by technical effects in the course of recording on tape.

All music was on tape. For the first time the accompaniments to the three songs – Ted Ragg's song poking fun at the delay, Greenwool's soppy 'Home Song' and Givola's 'Whitewash Song' – were all reproduced from tape.

[Ibid., pp. 147–8, 'Probennotat,' and p. 150, 'Die Musik'. In this production Ekkehard Schall played Ui: an outstanding performance. The music was by the Ensemble's musical director Hans-Dieter Hosalla.]

SONGS FOR THE BERLINER ENSEMBLE PRODUCTION

1. Ragg's Song

There was a little man
He had a little plan.
They told him to go easy
Just wait, my little man.
But waiting made him queasy.
    Heil Ui!
For he wants what he wants right now!

[Derived from the 'Was-man-hat-hat-man Song' in scene 7 of *The Round Heads and the Pointed Heads*, GW *Stücke*, p. 993.]

2. Greenwool's Song

A cabin stands beside the meadow
It used to be my happy home.
Now strangers' eyes are looking out the window
Oh, why did I begin to roam?
Home, take me home
Back to my happy home!
Home, take me home
Back to my happy home!

[Origin uncertain. Not by Brecht.]

3. Whitewash Song

When the rot sets in, when walls and roof start dripping
Something must be done at any price.
Now the mortar's crumbling, bricks are slipping.
If somebody comes it won't be nice.

But whitewash will do it, fresh whitewash will do it.
When the place caves in 'twill be too late.
Give us whitewash, boys, then we'll go to it
With our brushes till we fix things up first-rate.
Now, here's a fresh disaster
This damp patch on the plaster!
That isn't nice. (No, not nice.)
Look, the chimney's falling!
Really, it's appalling!
Something must be done at any price.
Oh, if only things would look up!
This abominable fuck-up
Isn't nice. (No, not nice.)
But whitewash will do it, lots of white will do it.
When the place caves in 'twill be too late.
Give us whitewash, boys, then we'll go to it
And we'll whitewash till we've got it all first-rate.
Here's the whitewash, let's not get upset!
Day and night we've got the stuff on hand.
This old shack will be a palace yet.
You'll get your New Order, just as planned.

[GW *Stücke*, tr. by Ralph Manheim, p. 936. This song origina-
ted as an appendage to Brecht's treatment ('The Bruise') for
The Threepenny Opera film, and was then taken into *The Round
Heads and the Pointed Heads*, where it is sung to a setting by
Hanns Eisler as an interlude between scenes 2 and 3.]

Editorial Note

Though *Ui* was among the most quickly written of all Brecht's plays we know little about its antecedents in his fertile mind. He himself spoke of it (in a journal entry for March 10, 1941) as inspired by thoughts of the American theatre and harking back to his New York visit of 1935, when he no doubt was made particularly aware of the Chicago gangs of the prohibition era and the films made about them by such firms as Warner Brothers and First National. The highly un-American name *Ui*, however, and its application to a Hitler-type leader, evidently originated slightly earlier when he was planning his never-finished prose work about the Tui's or Tellect-Ual-Ins, upside-down intellectuals whose ineffectiveness allowed such leaders to come to power. Walter Benjamin, making one of his visits to Brecht in Denmark in September 1934, noted that in addition to this more ambitious work Brecht was then writing a satire called *Ui* 'on Hitler in the style of a Renaissance historian'. This materialized in an unfinished and untitled short story set in classical Italy and describing an upstart city boss of Padua named Giacomo Ui, which can be found among Brecht's collected stories. Its style is deadpan, somewhat like that of the Julius Caesar novel which followed; its content is virtually the story of Hitler transposed into Roman terms. It resembles the eventual play in its depiction of the boss's rages, his aggressive ambitions, his currying of popular favour and even the way in which

> he was taught how to speak and walk by an old actor who had once in his heyday been permitted to play the mighty Colleone, and accordingly also taught him the latter's famous way of standing with his arms folded across his chest.

But the eight short sections of this story hardly get beyond establishing the character, and nothing is said about Hindenburg, the Reichstag Fire trial and the murder of Ernst Röhm, let alone the territorial annexations which were still to come. There are, however, several allusions to that anti-Semitism which the play curiously ignores (as do the notes on it) but which formed a major theme of another play in mock-Elizabethan style dating from 1934–35, *The Round Heads and the Pointed Heads* (which had itself developed out of an adaptation of *Measure for Measure* begun before 1933).

For years the three threads of gang warfare, the Ui-Hitler satire, and the elevated Elizabethan style, seem to have lain loosely coiled at the back of Brecht's mind before finally coming together in the spring of 1941. A further element may have been the example of Chaplin's *The Great Dictator*, even though Brecht could hardly yet have seen the actual film. On March 10 he roughed out a plan for ten or eleven scenes; by March 29 the first typescript was complete; after which Margarete Steffin drove him to tighten up the blank verse, another fortnight's work (all this according to his journal). The complete play, virtually in its present form, was ready about a month before the Brechts set out on their trip to the United States, whose imminence had of course helped to prompt it. There is thus much less than usual in the way of alternative scripts and versions, most of the revisions, such as they were, having been made directly on the first type-script. Many of them are primarily concerned with the iambic metre of the verse.

However, it appears that the Cauliflower Trust originally contained another member called Reely, who appeared in lieu of Butcher in scene 2. Dogsborough's first appearance was to have been in his city office, not in the homely surroundings of his restaurant, an amendment on the first script. In scene 3 Ui's first speech was shorter, the present version only having been established since the play's appearance in *Stücke IX* in 1957, when not all Brecht's amendments were available. The first three lines were as now, down to 'Is fame in such a place,' after which the speech concluded

> Two months without a brawl
> And twenty shoot-outs are forgotten, even
> In our own ranks!

There were also differences in the wording of Roma's speech which follows, though its sense was similar. In Scene 6, with the

old actor, Ui's and Givola's prose speeches were broken into
irregular verse lines, and it was an afterthought to have Ui take
over the Mark Antony speech from the actor and deliver most of
it solo. The name 'Dockdaisy' too was an afterthought; to start
with she was simply 'Mrs. Bowl' or 'the Person'. Clark's speech
in scene 7, showing the trust's solidarity with Ui and his gang,
was added at some point after the first script, together with Ui's
ensuing speech down to where Clark is heard to applaud it
(pp. 50–51). Then in the trial scene the playing of Chopin's
Funeral March on the organ was an afterthought on the first
script, as were all references to Giri's habit of wearing his
murdered victims' hats (which echoes an incident at the beginning
of *Happy End*, written in 1929). The first script ends with the
woman's speech later shifted to scene 9 (i.e., immediately prior to
the interval in the Berliner Ensemble production), this shift
having been made after the play's publication in 1957. The
epilogue was not in the first script.

When the play was finally staged by Palitzsch and Wekwerth in
1959 further changes were made, which were not included in the
published text but were meant to take account of the changed
public understanding of the historical background. According to
Wekwerth, Brecht himself was long chary of staging this play in
view of 'the German audience's lack of historical maturity'; he
did not allow his younger collaborators even to read it until the
summer before he died. They had to treat it as confidential, nor
was it to be produced until they had first staged *Fear and Misery
of the Third Reich* as an introduction to the tragic circumstances
which it satirized. Thus warned, and well aware of the type of
criticism voiced by Lothar Kusche (p. 109), the two directors
now set to work to implicate Dogsborough and the industrialists
more closely with Ui and to discourage German audiences from
sympathizing with Roma. Ui accordingly was not referred to in
scene 1a, and only entered the play once Sheet had refused to sell
his shipping business in 1b. Dogsborough's packet of shares was
given to him, not sold, while in scene 7 instead of seeming merely
passive he was seen actually to give Ui his support. The episode
with Goodwill and Gaffles was cut (pp. 34–36), to be replaced by
a new section stressing the involvement of heavy industry. Roma
was made to murder the journalist Ted Ragg, and scene 14 with

his Banquoesque ghost was omitted; he still, however, emerged as a good deal less unpleasant than Giri and Givola. The name of Chicago was replaced by Capua or Capoha throughout. Finally an extra song was introduced, the 'Whitewash Song' from *The Round Heads and the Pointed Heads*, which Givola sang after the interval (pp. 116–7).

The main interest of the scripts, however, lies rather in the evidence which they give of Brecht's intentions with regard to the play. The title varies: once or twice it is simply *The Rise of Arturo Ui*, while the copy formerly belonging to Elisabeth Hauptmann is headed '*Arturo Ui*. Dramatic Poem. By K. Keuner' – Mr. Keuner (or Mr. Naobody) being the alter ego who features in Brecht's prose aphorisms, as well as figuring as a character in two of the unfinished plays. Elsewhere Brecht referred to *Ui* as 'the gangster play,' a title which he also tried rendering into English as *The Gangster Play We Know* or again *That Well-known Racket*. There is a table too, giving what he calls 'The Parallels', to wit:

Dogsborough = Hindenburg
Arturo Ui = Hitler
Giri = Göring
Roma = Röhm
Givola = Goebbels
Dullfeet = Dollfuss
Cauliflower Trust = Junkers (or East Prussian landowners)
Vegetable dealers = Petty bourgeoisie
Gangsters = Fascists
Dock aid scandal = 'Osthilfe' [East Aid] scandal
Warehouse-fire trial = Reichstag Fire trial
Chicago = Germany
Cicero = Austria

– Röhm having been Captain Ernst Röhm, chief of staff of the brownshirted S.A. or main Nazi private army, who was murdered in the 'Night of the Long Knives' in June 1934, while the Osthilfe scandal related to a controversial pre-1933 subsidy to the Junkers. There are also slightly varying versions of the historical analogies provided by the projected 'inscriptions'. Thus in the first script the inscription following scene 4 read:

In January 1933 President Hindenburg more than once refused to appoint Party Leader Hitler as Reich Chancellor. He was, however, nervous of the proposed investigation of the so-called 'Osthilfe' scandal. Moreover he had accepted state money for the Neudeck estate presented to him, but failed to use it for its intended objective.

After scene 8, the trial, there was a now-omitted inscription which read:

When Reich Chancellor Schleicher threatened to expose the tax evasions and misappropriation of 'Osthilfe' money, Hindenburg on 30 January 1933 gave power to Hitler. The investigation was suppressed.

That after scene 13 read as follows:

The occupation of Austria was preceded by the murder of Engelbert Dollfuss, the Austrian Chancellor. Tirelessly the Nazis continued their efforts to win Austrian sympathies.

– and the final inscription simply:

Perhaps there is something else that could stop him?

Further light on the play's topical meaning is given by the photographs stuck into the pages of Brecht's first script. Scene 2, with Dogsborough, is followed by a portrait of Hindenburg, scene 3 by a drawing of gangsters captioned 'Murder Inc.' In scene 6, with the old actor, there are four pictures of Hitler in his characteristic attitude with the hands clasped before the private parts, followed by two more with the arms folded and one captioned 'Hitler the Orator'. A further picture of Hitler speaking precedes the trial scene (8). In scene 10, following Givola's forgery of Dogsborough's will, there is a photograph of Hitler and Goebbels going over a document together, then at the end one of Hitler and Göring shaking hands. Scene 11 (the garage) is preceded by a picture showing Göring and Goebbels in uniform, while in scene 13 (Dullfeet's funeral) there is a photograph of a gangster funeral in Chicago.